The ART of COUNSELLING

HUMAN HORIZONS SERIES

REVISED EDITION

The ART
of COUNSELLING
by
Rollo May

A CONDOR BOOK
SOUVENIR PRESS (E&A) LTD

First published in the U.S.A. by
Gardner Press, New York

First British Edition published 1992 by
Souvenir Press (Educational & Academic) Ltd.,
43 Great Russell Street London WC1B 3PA

Reprinted 1993, 1995

ISBN 0 285 65099 8

Printed in Great Britain by
The Guernsey Press Co. Ltd., Guernsey, Channel Islands

To
BOB AND ROGER AND LEE
and others of my counselees whose
personalities cross and recross the pages
of this book

Preface

A FRIEND WHO had taken a position teaching graduate students in education remarked that he and his class had sought a central book for students in his classes. These students did not want to become trained professional therapists but they did want to know the rudiments of the counseling that every teacher needs to do. "We could find no suitable book," my friend added "so we went back to your *Art of Counseling*."

This book has for me a fateful background. In the early thirties, I had come back from teaching for three years in central Europe, where, in the summer vacation, I had taken a seminar with Alfred Adler in Vienna. On returning to this country in the midst of the Great Depression, I had the good fortune to get a job called Advisor to Men Students at Michigan State University. This tripartite position included teaching a course at the university, advising students in the "Y," and overseeing student activities in the Interdenominational People's Church across the street from the university in which I had my office.

In those days Freud, Jung, Adler, Rank, and other psychotherapists were not taught in universities and were almost unknown in this country. Thus my contact with Adler turned out to be surprisingly useful. Persons with jobs similar to mine around the country were hungry for information about the procedures of counseling, and hence I was often invited to speak at conferences. Since there was nothing written in the field, or at least that we could find, I was urged to publish the lectures. The result was the original *Art of Counseling*, the first book on counseling produced in America.

In our modern day, strange to say, this "middle ground" is still largely uncovered. Libraries are full of books on "pop" psychology, and there is no dearth of books for those interested in the profession of intensive psychotherapy. The crying need is for those who do not wish to be psychotherapists but do need to know something about the inner workings of personality. This need is felt by others than those in education—physicians who often need to counsel the bereaved and to confer with patients on intimate topics, lawyers who are engaged in counseling clients, and so on, not to mention the obvious fields of religion and social work. Even members of corporations wish for knowledge about how to deal helpfully with people who work for them.

Hence, when Gardner Press proposed this revision, I agreed. This edition of the *Art of Counseling* has been almost completely revised, and I hope in language that will do justice to the significance of the topic and the fascination of the field.

ROLLO MAY

Contents

"The unexamined life is not worth living."
SOCRATES

"I saw that all the things I feared had nothing good or bad in them save as the mind was affected by them."
SPINOZA

He's a real nowhere man,
Sitting in his nowhere land,
Making all his nowhere plans for nobody.

Doesn't have a point of view,
Knows not where he's going to,
Isn't he a bit like you and me?

Nowhere man, please listen,
You don't know what you're missing,
Nowhere man, the world is at your command.
LENNON & MCCARTNEY

PART

ONE

Underlying Principles

I
A Picture
of Personality

WHAT IS A human being? Here our constructive discussion must begin, for the effectiveness of counseling with human beings depends upon our understanding of what those human beings really are. A man is more than his body, more than his job, more than his social position, and a woman is more than a mother, more than her attractiveness, or her work. These are but aspects through which they express themselves. The totality of this expression is the external mirror of that inner structure which we call, somewhat vaguely, "personality." European psychologists would use the term "soul" in this connection as a translation of "psyche," but for us in America the word "personality" expresses more accurately that basic nature of a human being which makes him or her a person.

So we must begin by determining a concept of personality. The counselor who neglects doing this consciously will do it nevertheless unconsciously—unwittingly working on the assumption, for example, that the counselee should develop a personality just like the counselor's own, or like that of the counselor's particular hero, or like the personality ideal of the particular culture. The wise counselor will not leave this basic matter to the vagaries of unconsciousness, but will consciously and reasonably draw up a picture of personality.

For the sake of clarity let us state our conclusion before we begin; namely, that personality is characterized by *freedom, individuality, social integration,* and *religious tension.* These are the four principles, as the following discussion will indicate, that are essential to human personality. To make a more complete definition, it could be stated that personality is an actualization of the life process in a free individual who is socially integrated and is aware of spirit.

1
Is Personality Determined?

The deterministic picture of personality is represented most vividly and persuasively in Freudian psychoanalysis. Unquestionably Freud will go down in history as one of the most influential thinkers of our century. He is a watershed in the history of our endeavor to understand ourselves. Indeed, Freud has robbed mankind of the luxury of being hypocritical and dishonest—which partly explains why he has been so bitterly attacked.*

Freud was born into an age that was calling for psychoanalysis. The nineteenth century had so parceled up human nature, had so compartmentalized life and reduced moral living to a matter

---

*The reader is referred to the brief historical survey of the psychotherapeutic movement. See Note 1, page 173.

of superficial decisions, that Freud's psychoanalysis was greatly needed. Only in the light of our need can the wide influence of psychoanalysis be explained. Freud came to show us that there was much more to personality than our little systems had allowed. He discovered the "depth" in human nature as contained in the profound and powerful realms of the unconsciousness. His centering upon sex as the most influential of human instincts, while too extreme a position to be true in detail, is an inevitable reaction from the hypocritical Victorian moralism that had assumed it could ignore the sex factor in life, cut it out and throw it away, and then go blithely on in "innocence."

In his exploration among human motives in the unconsciousness, Freud dug up much that was too ugly to be palatable to a generation that had tried to settle all questions in the "immediate center of decision," shelving moral matters by the signing of cards and international problems by the signing of treaties. Freud showed us the ugly side of human nature. Anyone who still believes that human nature does not have an ugly side— represented in primitive lusts and savage cruelties—has only to look at the war-torn state of the modern world. Our narcissism has led us to condemn Freud as a purveyor of slander and smut; but "it is only a great idealist," as Jung says, "who could have given his life to the uncovering of so much dirt."

Freud was an analytical genius. And he invented a system for analyzing human personality, called psychoanalysis, which teaches counselors much of value about the function of the human mind.[1] He observed that the adjustments within the individual's mind can be thrown into chaotic disorder by "repressions." These repressions actually represent the individual's being dishonest with himself or herself. The process is somewhat as follows: An instinctual urge pushes up from the "id" (the seething cauldron in the unconsciousness of desires and fears and instinctual tendencies and every sort of psychic content) and seeks expression in the outside world. But the ego, which stands at the threshold of consciousness and mediates between the id and the outside world, is aware of society's prohibitions against the expression of this particular desire, and so it resorts to some ruse to repress the desire. The ruse is a trick by which the ego says to itself, "I don't want to express this desire anyway," or "I'll do this instead." But the repression only means that the urge will come pushing out again in another form—this time in some neurotic syndrome such as anxiety or embarrassment or forgetfulness or even some more serious form of psychosis.

When a neurotic patient comes to treatment with a Freudian psychoanalyst, the analyst sets the patient to verbalizing associations, which is called "free association." During this "confession," as it is termed, the analyst lies in wait for signs of a repression, such as the patient's hesitating at some crucial point or forgetting or showing pronounced embarrassment. Such inhibitions or blockages indicate a disunity in the patient's mind, a lack of ready flow from the unconscious source of instinctual tendencies into the consciousness and thence into reality. These symptoms are buoys that indicate the existence of psychological conflicts underneath. Now it becomes the function of the analyst to track down this conflict, to bring it out of the unconsciousness into plain sight, and, if it is serious, to relieve it by a process of psychological catharsis called abreaction. The end result is to disentangle the patient's mental snarls, to free the patient from the "complex," and thus to reestablish some functional unity in the mind.

This liberates the patient to work out some more satisfactory expression of instinctual urges in reality. Or if expression is impossible, the patient at least is brought to accept consciously and frankly the necessity for renunciation. The central process of psychoanalysis consists of bringing the conflict out of the dark unconsciousness into the light of consciousness where it can be recognized and reasonably handled. "Our usefulness," says Freud, "consists in replacing the unconscious by the conscious, in translating the unconscious into the conscious."[2]

Among the valuable contributions this system of psychoanalysis makes to our understanding of the human mind is, first, the insight it affords into the tremendous extent and potency of the realm of the unconscious. The exploration of this dark hinterland out of which arise the great forces and motives of life has placed our understanding of humans on a much sounder basis. Psychoanalysis shows, also, that we must take much more into our consideration than the conscious ego. This poor "general" has a precarious time of it at best, being buffeted about by the instinctual forces from the id, the outside world, and the superego (conscience). Living must therefore be oriented to far deeper levels than merely that of the conscious will. And finally, Freudian psychoanalysis proves that we can never succeed in the moral life by so simple a device as mere repression of every tendency society or our own superego finds unpalatable.

But the danger in the Freudian system of analysis arises when it is carried over into a deterministic interpretation of personality as a whole.[3] The system can become simply a scheme of cause and effect: blocked instinctual urge equals repression equals psychic complex equals neurosis. And the cure consists theoretically of merely reversing the process: observe the neurotic symptom, trace down the complex, remove the repression, and then assist the individual to a more satisfactory expression of instinctual urges. We do not mean to say that Freudian therapy as it is practiced is as simple as this; the therapy has many more creative aspects, and it succeeds precisely because it does not bind itself to the strict causological theory. The danger lies in the influence of Freudian theory in setting up a mechanistic, deterministic view of personality in the minds of the partially informed public, so that people conclude that they are the victims of their instinctual drives and that their only salvation lies in expressing their libido whenever the urge arises.

To be sure, the cause-and-effect system is valid for certain aspects of mind. But it is an error to draw generalizations from this limited area that imply that causological, deterministic principles explain the whole of personality. Freud was seduced by the handy, tangible systemization of natural science; and he used it as a Procrustean bed on which he laid the human personality and forced it to fit.[4] This fallacy arose out of a failure to recognize the limits of the scientific method. Though the objectivity of science aids us greatly in coming to a useful understanding of certain phases of human mental phenomena, to imagine that the whole of the creative, oftentimes unpredictable, certainly intangible, aspects of human mind can be reduced to cause-and-effect, mechanistic principles is sheer folly. Consequently Freud's "natural science psychology," as Rank called it, was led astray in its theories of ultimate determinism in personality.

If such a determinism is accepted, human responsibility is destroyed. The thief can say, "Not I but my hunger stole the apple." What of purpose and freedom and creative decision on the part of the individual? These things are basic in personality, as we shall observe below.

As a matter of fact, one of the basic presuppositions in all psychotherapy is that patients sooner or later must accept responsibility for themselves. Therefore, personal determinism, which excuses them from responsibility, works in the end directly against regaining mental health. Cause-and-effect determinism holds only for a limited area, namely, the area of the repression-complex neurosis; and when freed from the complex, the patient becomes responsible for creatively working out the patient's own future destiny.

Neurotic persons, in my experience, are often precisely the ones who tend to hold a deterministic outlook on life. They seek to blame something else for their difficulties—their parents, or their childhood environment, or their associates; "anything," they seem to be pleading, "so long as I am not to blame." This is understandable, for if they once admitted their own responsibility, they would be forced to take steps to overcome the neurosis. There are, of course, an infinite number of determining factors in any personality difficulty; but underneath all there lies in the individual's own autonomy a point of responsibility and possibility for creative development—and this is the significant factor.

A middle-aged man, manager of a small business in a village, with whom I recently dealt, was in the habit of arguing determinism with great vehemence. He cited experiments with monkeys and every sort of far-fetched pseudoscientific parallel, and seemed bent by hook or crook to prove that humans are no more responsible for their actions than were Pavlov's dogs for the appearance of saliva in their mouths when the appropriate stimulus was given. When one argues as though one's life depends on it, incidentally, you may be sure that more than objective interest in truth lies behind the passion. One is probably trying to save one's own neurotic scheme from disturbance. Sure enough, it turned out that this man had failed consistently in a number of jobs since graduating from college. He spoke of his college with embarrassment, and then only to point out that college education does one little good in life. This man, we may conclude, *had* to believe in determinism so long as he failed in his own life. It was his excuse; it relieved him of the oppressive burden of his sense of failure. He was determined to be a determinist *by his mistakes*. But the very vehemence of his arguing gave proof of his subconscious guilty feeling about his failures, and hence he argued determinism precisely because he had a deep conviction that he was not entirely determined.

Yes, determinism does operate in some cases, but these are the neurotic cases. Neurosis means a surrendering of freedom, a giving of one's self over to rigid training formulas; and consequently the personality does become a machine at that point. Mental health means a regaining of one's sense of personal responsibility, and hence of one's freedom.

2
Freedom of the Person

Freedom is a basic principle, in fact, a *sine qua non*, of personality. It is by this characteristic that we separate human beings from animals, the human being having the ability to break the rigid chain of stimulus and response that enslaves animals. The healthy mind is able to hold different impulses in a state of undecided balance and finally to make the decision by which one of the impulses prevails. This possession of creative possibilities, which is synonymous with freedom, is the first presupposition of human personality.

It is not our purpose here to delve into the philosophical proofs of human freedom, but only to point out that, from the psychological point of view, it is essential to believe in freedom in order to have an adequate picture of personality on which to do effective counseling. This ought not to be called "freedom of the will," as that implies that a particular *part* of a person is free, and it results in endless discussions about metaphysical determinism that get us nowhere.[5] Rather, a people possess freedom as a quality of their total being. This is not to say, let it be remembered, that there are not an infinite number of determining influences playing upon the individual from all sides at all moments—many more determining forces than the last century with its emphasis on simple "effort" ever realized. But regardless of how many determining forces affect John or Jane Doe, there is in the end an element by which Mr. or Ms. Doe molds the materials of heredity and environment into his or her own unique pattern. Arguing against freedom only proves it the more firmly; an argument, in fact, any sort of reasonable discussion or even the asking of questions, presupposes this margin of freedom.

Students often come to the counselor and defend a certain irresponsible point of view on the basis of smatterings of natural science to which they have been exposed sufficiently to see the force but not the limitations. If a personality problem is at stake, the counselor will not argue the question directly—counseling is never argument. But the counselor will point out possibilities, and thus gradually bring the student to an acceptance of responsibility for the student's conduct and future.

The psychotherapist Otto Rank definitively explained the importance of freedom and responsibility in psychotherapy.[6] Long one of Freud's closest associates, Rank was finally forced to break with the master because of Freud's refusal to admit the centrality of creative will in the psychoanalytic treatment.[7] Rank held that in the long run we must admit that one creates one's own personality by creative willing, and that neurosis is attributable precisely to the fact that the patient cannot will constructively.[8]

It is possible to grow in freedom. The more mentally healthy the person becomes, the more he or she is able to mold creatively the materials of life, and hence the more appropriate the potentiality of freedom. A counselor, therefore, who helps a counselee to overcome a personality difficulty has helped him or her to become more free.

To summarize our first principle of personality, freedom, in the form of a guide for counseling: *It is the function of the counselor to lead the counselee to an acceptance of responsibility for the conduct and outcome of his or her life*. The counselor will show the counselee how deep lie the roots of decision, how all previous experience and the forces of the unconscious must be reckoned with, but in the end will aid the counselee to appropriate and use his or her own possibilities for freedom.

3
Individuality in Personality

The second principle that is basic in personality is individuality. Persons who come to the counselor with personality problems have this difficulty because they cannot be themselves—cannot, in other words, individuate. "The neurotic type," Rank pertinently says, "which we all represent to a certain extent, suffers from the fact that he cannot accept himself, cannot endure himself, and will have it otherwise."[9]

In the end, one has only one's self through which to live and face the world. If people cannot be themselves, they certainly cannot assume any other self no matter how greatly they may wish to do so. Each self is different from every other self; it is unique, and healthiness of mind depends upon accepting this uniqueness.

Consider the infinite variety in persons! A crowd in a shopping mall appears to move like a stream of marbles, each person wearing the same poker face—but look beneath the protective mask and how wonderfully variegated and unique are the aspects of each individual! The counselor will be continually amazed by the uniqueness and originality of each story. Sometimes, after a fatiguing series of interviews, I find myself subconsciously assuming that I must have met all possible types of persons and that the next one will be only a boring repetition. But scarcely has this next one progressed but a few sentences when I realize that here is an exciting novel I have never read. One is overcome in wonder at nature's resourcefulness in creating them "male and female" and everyone different. The counselor feels like crying with the psalmist, "When I consider thy heavens, the work of thy fingers. . . . What is man? . . . . For thou has made him but little lower than God, and crownest him with glory and honor." It is this uniqueness of each person that we as counselors seek to preserve. The function of the counselor is to help the counselee be what destiny intended him or her to be.

The mistakes in life occur when individuals try to act some other role than their own. The student who inveterately says the wrong thing at social functions is not to be pigeonholed as inherently tactless, but may be possessed of an inner fear which makes the student try to act an alien role—and, of course, the result is blunder. Many instances of young people slipping into loose sexual practices are to be understood as a result of their fear of being themselves and their consequent desperate clutching at another role. Getting drunk, it is obvious, is a form of escaping one's self. When a young man gets "tight" before a party, he is arranging things so that he will not have to be himself at the party. The pertinent question is not, why does he drink too much? Rather, it is why does he feel he has to flee from himself? It follows that we should set up a social program for our young people in which they can be themselves and get satisfaction from it. Such social functions would be the best kind of exercise in personality health.

It is self-evident that psychotherapy works fundamentally on this principle of individuality. Rank explained it as the aim of his method: "To say it in one word, the aim is self-development; this is, the person is to develop himself into that which he is."[10]

The definitive statement on the subject of individuality comes from the renowned Swiss psychologist, Carl Jung. His work, *Psychological Types* was so pertinent to modern needs that his terms "introvert" and "extrovert" have become common parlance. Extroverts live in such a way as to correspond with objective conditions, or demands that originate outside themselves; they tend, like business people or soldiers, to emphasize activity.[11] Introverts, on the other hand, are oriented primarily to subjective data; poets and philosophers and lovers of scientific research tend to fall in this category. There is, of course, no hard and fast line; we all have more or less introvertive and extrovertive tendencies. Jung realized that his system, which he developed much more intricately than here indicated, is simply a frame of reference that gives very general pointer readings. It is neither right nor fruitful to pigeonhole people. Jung himself, significantly, was the psychotherapist who most emphasized individuality. It is helpful if we keep a very pliable frame of categories for reference, but let it be remembered that in the end there must be a unique category for every individual.

In America there is a tendency to identify extroversion with personality health and introversion with illness. We Americans tend to be extroverts because of our pioneer, activist background and our present preoccupation with business and industry, linked with an underemphasis, especially in the past, on cultural pursuits. This is the mischievous error of assuming that *our* particular type is the only healthy type. The youth who is essentially the artist, or the reflective philosopher, or the devotee of scientific research may be made psychologically unhealthy by being pushed into the position of a commercial salesperson. Of course the caution against becoming *too* introvertive is sound, and it is even more dangerous to be too introvertive than too extrovertive, for society can be depended upon to help beat the extrovert off any egocentric tangents. But the ultimate aim is that the individual find his or her own unique role.

The most vicious mistake many counselors make is in trying to compress their counselees into a particular type—usually the type to which the counselor belongs. The counselor did not join a fraternity in college, and so assumes it is better that the student not join. The professor studied very hard as an undergraduate, and so may advise the sophomore to let up on social activities and plunge into books. These are crude examples, but the point will be clear; namely, that there is always a vicious tendency for the counselor to view the counselee in terms of the counselor's own attitudes, moral standards, and general personality pattern, and consequently to project these upon the counselee, thus violating the autonomy of the counselee's individuality.

There is good ground, then, for the advice so often bandied about, "be yourself." But it does little good simply to tell one to be oneself, for the trouble is precisely that one does not know which self one really is. The counselee often feels a number of conflicting "selves," and to tell one merely to be oneself is to make confusion worse confounded. One must first *find* oneself—and this is where the counselor comes in.

The counselor's function is to help the counselee find what Aristotle speaks of as "entelechy," the unique form in the acorn which destines it to grow into an oak. "Each of us carries his own life-form," says Jung, "an indeterminable form which cannot be superseded by another."[12] This life form, the real self, reaches into depths in the individual's mind far below ordinary consciousness; consciousness may even present a distorted mirroring of it. One finds oneself by uniting one's conscious self with various levels of one's unconsciousness.

At this point it is necessary to describe and define more clearly this important realm of the unconscious. Everyone has experienced the fact that only a small portion of one's mental content is conscious at any given moment. Mental content moves through consciousness in a stream—like film moves in a reel across the light of a movie projector to throw an everchanging picture on the screen. The old simile has it that the conscious portion of mind compares with the unconscious as the tip of the iceberg rising out of the water compares with the much larger bulk of it floating under the surface. Certainly our minds reach infinitely deeper than any momentary area of consciousness—how deep we cannot determine, for unconscious means "unknown." We can only postulate the unconscious and observe how it manifests itself functionally. Persons who have become habituated to thinking only in the limited terms of calculable science sometimes hesitate to postulate the unconscious; but to do that is to cut off the great bulk of our mental life. What of all the memories, past experiences, knowledge, *ad infinitum* that are not in our conscious minds at this particular instant but which we could summon there at a moment's notice? No experience is ever lost, theoretically. Nothing is really forgotten, and childhood experiences leave their force upon the persons even though they may shrug their shoulders and think the matter lost and gone forever. Memory and forgetfulness and other problems of the unconscious are intricate matters, and there is still much knowledge to be gained about them.

Our functional interpretation pictures the unconscious as a great storehouse including every sort of psychic content: fears, hopes, desires, and all kinds of instinctual tendencies. But it is a dynamo even more than a storehouse, for out of it come the drives and tendencies which consciousness merely directs. "The great decisions of life," Jung rightly said, "have as a rule far more to do with the instincts and other mysterious unconscious factors than with the conscious will and well-meaning reasonableness."[13]

The unconscious may be viewed as a series of levels. This concept corresponds to actual experience, for an experience of childhood seems to be much "deeper" than one of yesterday. Freud spoke of the "preconscious" as that portion of the unconscious just below consciousness. We may term this preconsciousness material that can rise immediately to consciousness, plus childhood experiences and repressed material, the "personal unconscious."

As we plumb deeper into the unconscious, we find more and more material which the individual possesses in common with other individuals. Jung gave the useful term "collective unconscious" to these deeper levels. The French or citizens of the United States, for example, hold much material in their unconscious which they did not experience themselves, but which they absorb from their national groups. This will have a certain connection with the history of their nation, but it is transmitted in much deeper ways than through history classrooms and text-books. The pioneer experiences of early Americans carry through with some force into the unconscious of a modern American, though the latter is several generations removed from the actual pioneer life. In primitive societies where the collective con-sciousness is greater, it is quite difficult to tell where the ex-periences of the forebears leave off and those of the present begin. An even deeper stratum of the unconscious is that which we possess in common with all other members of our race, or deeper still, that held collectively by members of the western world.

And, finally, there are certain patterns in the unconscious which the individual possesses in common with all humankind. Jung calls these "archetypes" or "primordial images"—defined as the patterns or ways of thought which persons possess simply because they are human. These archetypes have a relationship to the basic structure of mind. This explains why mythology, though springing up among peoples of diverse races and periods in history, exhibits common patterns.

Is the collective unconscious inherited or acquired from one's culture? Jung's answer is direct: "We mean by collective un-conscious, a certain psychic deposition shaped by the forces of heredity."[14] As a matter of fact, the source of the collective un-conscious is not the pertinent problem; we observe how it works functionally, and it certainly is true from this viewpoint that these basic ideas, as they appear even in the mythological creations of children, come from something deeper and more organic than what the individual could have learned from his or her educators. Specific ideas, of course, are acquired from one's environment, and we are not arguing here that all human ideas are "innate." But there must be something structural in mind comparable to the structural form of body which would develop along certain general lines even though the individual were isolated on Crusoe's island. Plato was wrestling with this same difficult problem of describing the function of the collective unconscious when he ex-plained, mythologically, that man is born with certain ideas which carry over from his previous existence in heaven. And so Plato held knowledge to be a reminiscence or a process of tapping what is already deep in one's unconscious.[15]

Great poetry and art and philosophy and religion spring out of this collective unconscious of humanity. The great artist, like Aeschylus or Dante or Shakespeare, taps these deep levels of human sorrow and joy and fear and hope, and serves as an artesian well through which eternal patterns spring into expression.[16] A classic in literature or art is the expression of psychic images which the individual possesses in common with all other human beings. Later we shall discuss the implications of the locating of religion in the collective unconscious. Here let us only note that "conscience" is given a new validity. Conscience is something more than a residue of one's parents' teachings, more than an expression of social solidarity; it reaches far back into the mysterious sources of our being.

To get back to the individual who comes to the counselor with a personality difficulty. That person needs to find his or her true self, and this is accomplished by arriving at some degree of unity of consciousness with the unconscious levels of childhood experience, the deeper levels of the collective unconscious, and ultimately with that source of his mind which is in the very structure of the universe. It now becomes clear why the neurotic individual can never be healthy while blaming childhood training for the trouble, as the person *is* to some extent that childhood training, and in fighting it is fighting himself or herself. Likewise, individuals who are continually at war with society can never attain personality health, for they are struggling against certain forces in the collective unconscious of their own minds.

Finally, they who struggle against the universe, who deny meaning in the universe and try to break off connection with it actually are struggling against the deepest point in themselves, where they are connected with the universe. This is another way of saying that the individual has the roots of his or her collective unconscious in that creative structure of the universe which are infinite. In dueling against Infinity, one is actually stabbing the rapier into the deepest portions of one's own soul. Discussion of this important matter must be reserved for the final chapter.

Suffice it to say here that when individuals truly find themselves, they find their society and they find their roots in the spiritual sources of the universe.

From the second principle of personality, individuality, we derive this guide for counseling: *It is the function of the counselor to assist the counselee to find his true self, and then to help him or her to have courage to be this self.*

II

The Search for One's Self

PERSONALITY CANNOT BE understood apart from its social setting. This social setting—the community of other persons—gives personality a world without which it would have no meaning. The social setting furnishes the pegs to which personality attaches the lines of tension of its web, to carry through the simile of the last chapter. We know this to be true in our own experience, for each of us uses other persons as pivot points; we pivot around our enemies as well as around our friends.

1

Social Integration

Thus the third aspect of healthy personality is *social integration*. So important is this aspect that people have fallen into the habit of assuming that personality difficulty means social difficulty, and that an individual who is a social success must have solved any personality problems. This, of course, presupposes a superficial view of personality—as when the word is profaned in cosmetic and "how-to-be-a-social-success" advertisements. But profoundly viewed, a meaningful social adjustment is basic in personality, for the person must move in a world that consists of other people.

A chief characteristic of the neurotic is an inability to get along with other people. He or she is highly suspicious of others, feels society to be an enemy, and moves through life as though in an armored car. A man recently explained to me that he had spent his vacation trying to get away from his relatives, and then remarked incidentally, "I never trust anyone." Even though this is a common remark, it is a bona fide sign of a neurotic attitude toward society. Such an individual is bound to be lonely, as he forces himself into as isolated and comfortless a position as a machine gunner fighting all for himself on a mountain top.

In this matter of social integration, we are most indebted to Alfred Adler,[1] that other Viennese who, with Freud, made Vienna the mother city of psychotherapy. Dr. Adler noticed in his early psychological work in the first years of this century that the neurotic is especially characterized by an inability to make connections with other people and the social world. Adler observed, too, that no one can separate oneself from one's social group and remain healthy, as the very structure of one's personality is dependent upon the community. The child would not have been born except for a social act on the part of its parents, and it could not have survived a day without the care of the family. At any given instant, every individual is dependent upon countless other persons of the present and every previous time. To get a vivid glimpse of this social interdependence, simply call to mind the long train of persons upon whom you are dependent for the bread on your dinner table, or for your ability to say the multiplication table. We live in a social constellation in which every individual is dependent upon every other individual just as the stars in the solar constellations hang upon the lines of gravitational force emanating from every other heavenly body. In fact, this web of interdependence theoretically includes every individual who lives or ever lived. Even a person who denies this interdependence and fights against it, like Nietzsche, is still dependent on it in the very act of attacking it. The sense of interdependence is continually cropping up out of the collective unconscious of the misanthropic individual who refuses to admit it consciously. Adler calls this interdependence the "love and logic which bind us all together."

As opposed to Freud's concept of sex libido, Adler sees the dynamic force in the individual as a striving for power. There is an urge within the individual (in the center of the self we term the "ego") to gain superiority over others, to attain a position of security which cannot be threatened.[2] This is similar to, but not identical with, the "will to power" concepts of such philosophers as Nietzsche and Schopenhauer, but Adler's "will" is more a "will to prestige." It is that basic impulse that makes the individual tend to break out of the web of social interdependence and set himself or herself, by competitive ambition and vanity, above his or her peers.[3]

This brings us to the most famous contribution of Adlerian psychology to modern thought, the concept of inferiority. The inferiority feeling (it should not be called "complex" until it has become definitely neurotic) is universal. Every individual has it as part of being human. John Doe feels inferior to the people around him at a social function and is embarrassed (he forgets that they, too, feel inferior to him). The Browns feel inferior to the Joneses across the street, and hence the great striving to "keep up with the Joneses." Saleswoman Black has a feeling of inferiority about her job and so becomes jealous of others' successes; and the business world, shot through with everyone's effort to climb over the others, becomes a melee of merciless competition. It is surprising what Olympian forms the inferiority feeling assumes. The dog who is afraid, Aesop would say, is the one who barks most ferociously.

This universal inferiority feeling has its roots in the real inferiority of the infant, who sees adults exerting power which it lacks. It is also traceable in part to the real inferiority of primitive people as they strove against animals. Tooth for tooth and claw for claw, humans were easy prey for animals; and hence it was necessary that they compensate for physical weakness with mental agility. The development of civilization is to be understood to some extent as compensatory; that is, a result of mankind's striving to overcome inferiority.

Since we all have the inferiority feeling, it is not to be considered abnormal in itself. Indeed, coupled with the will to prestige, it furnishes us with our main source of motive power. The problem is to utilize this power, not in antisocial striving which destroys the social constellation, but in constructive effort which contributes to the well-being of others.

But an exaggerated inferiority feeling leads to neurotic behavior because it gives the ego an abnormally strong striving for power. The more "under" or minus the individual feels, the more desperately will that person struggle to be "on top." The inferiority feeling and the will to prestige are merely two aspects of the same drive within the individual. Thus we can infer that behind a tremendous ambition there lurks a deep (though possibly unconscious) inferiority feeling. Historical instances prove this time and again. What is called a "superiority complex" is for the same reason merely the reverse side of an underlying inferiority feeling —because the ego feels itself inferior, it assumes a special front of superiority and makes sure that everyone notices it.

In this scheme of striving for prestige, the lowering of other persons is equivalent to the raising of the individual; as they go down, one automatically gains more superiority. This explains why people derive pleasure from gossiping. Everyone has felt this tendency to lower others for the sake of the raising of their own prestige. The normal individual keeps the tendency under control, and aims to direct such efforts socially; but the neurotic directs such striving antisocially and attempts to climb up a ladder made of other persons—thus warring against the very structure to which the neurotic owes his or her existence. Such persons cut away their own roots, which cannot help ending in mental ill-health. Adler, therefore, defines neurosis as antisocial striving for power.

The chief human sins, which are, according to Adler, continually destroying human culture and happiness, are *vanity* and *ambition*, the two expressions of the dominating ego. Americans may find it difficult to see why ambition, which we consider a virtue, should be called a sin. What Adler actually means, however, is "antisocial ambition"; and we must agree with him that exaggerated ambition, as it is manifested in the historic conquerors or modern captains of industry, is rooted in the ego's striving for power rather than in the desire to serve humanity.

The normal striving for power should be differentiated from the neurotic. Normal ambition proceeds from strength, is a natural function of the living being, and is not necessarily antisocial; neurotic ambition proceeds from weakness and insecurity, and derives its satisfaction from the debasing and dominating of others.

This brings home the need for courage in healthy living. When individuals are given courage, they are relieved from the compulsion of inferiority feeling and therefore do not need to strive against others. Fear creates great havoc in human relations. The misanthropic, given basic courage, is suddenly relieved of much of his or her insecurity and able to cooperate with the group.

In addition to courage, the highest virtues, according to the Adlerian system, are *social interest* and *cooperation*. These mark healthy individuals who realize and cheerfully accept social responsibility. By expressing themselves in socially constructive ways, they are able to achieve and realize themselves, whereas misanthropic individuals "seeking to save their lives" in egocentric striving actually lose them. Healthy individuals become socially "integrated," which literally means attaining "wholeness." They "renew" their primordial position as an organic part of community, and thus are relieved from neurotic anxieties and little fears and inhibitions. "Only that individual can go through life without anxiety," says Adler, "who is conscious of belonging to the fellowship of man."[4]

Does the second aspect of personality, individuality, militate against social integration? Not ideally. As Shakespeare put it:

"To thine own self be true,
And it must follow, as the night the day,
Thou canst not then be false to any man."

Superficially, it is true, there may be a tension between individuality and social integration; to get along with one's neighbors, one often has to inhibit certain superficial expressions of individuality. But more profoundly speaking there is not the incompatibility between individuality and social living that people often assume; in the collective unconscious we are united with others even within ourselves.[5] It is true that there is an egocentric element which makes it very difficult for humans to be genuinely social, as will be discussed later; but this egocentric element also destroys their unity within the self. Practically speaking, counselors will find that the more socially integrated the counselee becomes, the more, on the whole, he or she will realize unique individuality.

From the third principle of personality, social integration, we derive this guide for counseling: *It is the counselor's function to assist the counselee to a cheerful acceptance of social responsibility, to give courage which will release the counselee from the compulsion of inferiority feeling, and to help the counselee to direct his or her striving toward socially constructive ends.*

2
The Source of Spirit

Earlier in this chapter, we spoke of the psychoanalytic view that mental illness consists of a disunity in the mind of the patient and the psychological conflicts which follow from this. And we mentioned that the aim of psychoanalysis was to reunify mental life by bringing the conflict out of the unconscious into consciousness.

This emphasis of psychoanalysis upon mental unity has been taken by many people to mean that the more unity one can achieve in one's personality the healthier one is, that the ideal is a final unity, and that psychological conflicts are therefore unhealthy in themselves. The Jungian emphasis upon the unifying of the individual's consciousness with various substrata in his or her unconscious and the Adlerian goal of integration of the individual with society likewise lend themselves to the interpretation that a unity within the mind of the individual is the ultimate goal.

It is perfectly true that the neurotic person suffers from a breakdown in unity of mental functions, and it is likewise self-evident that guiding the person back to a more effective adjustment with its accompanying condition of new unity is a step in the cure. But it is not true that a simple and ultimate unity within personality is the ideal. The amateur devotees of psychotherapy, and a portion of the public at large who have a smattering of the ideas of psychoanalysis, misinterpret psychotherapy and over-simplify personality when they assume that the goal is a state of complete relaxation, in which one can readily express all instinctual desires in reality and live the life of the lotus eaters or the inhabitants of the Mohammedan heaven. Some people tend to think that the aim of psychotherapy is to put everyone into a Garden of Eden where all urges are satisfied and one wanders about in a bliss which is undisturbed by moral and psychological conflict. All this is, of course, quite foreign to the human situation, and no reputable psychotherapist would admit such an ideal.

A final unity in the human personality is neither possible nor desirable. Existence in the Garden of Eden or in the heavens of the blissful and placid type would mean death to personality as we know it. For personality is dynamic, not static; creative, not vegetative. What we desire is a new and constructive adjustment of tensions rather than any final unity. We do not wish to wipe away conflict altogether—that would be stagnation—but rather *to transform destructive conflicts into constructive ones.*

It must be admitted that the psychotherapists have given room for this popular misinterpretation to develop. Freud did it in his natural science presuppositions and his tendency to reduce personality to cause-and-effect determinism. Adler similarly erred in his rationalistic faith in the idea that knowledge will lead to virtue. There are certain rationalistic, romantic, naturalistic presuppositions underlying the historical development of psychotherapy which lend themselves to this oversimplification. The temptation is to view personality as something which grows as simply and naturally as plants, as is illustrated in the remark of a therapist of the Adlerian school who defined the function of psychotherapy: "To remove the obstructions from the path of the personality as you remove the stones obstructing the growth of a flower, thus letting the flower grow up naturally toward the sun." Such a confidence in the natural growing of the human being toward a perfect state reminds us of Rousseau, and it is certainly to be viewed as a romantic faith lacking sufficient realism.

This tendency toward oversimplification is evidenced in the handling of the problem of *guilt feeling*. Some psychotherapists aim to wipe away guilt feeling entirely, treating it as a symptom of mental ill health, and reproaching religion for increasing the morbid guilt feeling of many people. To be sure, they are right in the respect that exaggerated guilt feeling is often connected with neurosis, and also that unenlightened religion has altogether too often abetted morbid guilt feeling in its adherents. An example is the case of a minister who was burdened for twenty-seven years by an obsession of sin which turned out in the end to be purely subjective and without relation to any reality. It is quite understandable that Freud, specializing in sexual phenomena, should treat guilt feeling as unhealthy, because the nineteenth century had attached a tremendous amount of morbid guilt to sexual phenomena.[6] Psychotherapists and counselors will unite in the endeavor to free people from morbid guilt feeling.

But guilt feeling can never be wiped away entirely, nor would it be desirable to do so. Guilt feeling is often the reverse side of one's sense of spirit, and in this sense it can be healthy and constructive.

Guilt feeling is *perception of the difference between what a thing is and what it ought to be*. Everyone experiences a guilt feeling an infinite number of times a day. When one passes a cripple begging on the street or a drunk in the gutter, when by neglect or conscious deed one does harm to another person, when one is aware of war going on even in another country—in short, one experiences guilt feeling whenever one has a feeling of "ought," a sense of the discrepancy between what is and what ought to be, or what one does and what one ought to do, or what the situation is and what it ought to be. This should not be confused with "conscience"—guilt feeling is the much broader aspect of human experience of which conscience is one expression. In the example of the beggar, the guilt feeling does not depend on whether or not one gives the beggar money: it may be sociologically better not to give; but the feeling of guilt inheres in the realization that here is a situation—a human being degraded into begging—which is far from any norm or ideal of human living.

If there were any act in life in which the individual could attain unity in self and thus transcend the guilt feeling, it would be the act of pure creativity such as occurs in that most intense moment in painting when the artist is carried up into a kind of ecstacy. But artists very often have the most poignant and vivid feeling of guilt about their work. While an artist is intensely engrossed in painting, the creative process seems to grasp and carry him or her along like a chip on a wave with such speed that he or she is for the moment conscious of nothing outside the creative act itself. But when the picture is finished, the artist has two emotions: one is the satisfaction and the sense of psychological catharsis which all creative effort brings; the other is the guilt feeling, bathed and made even more distinct in outline by the catharsis. This guilt feeling is first a realization that the picture is not as perfect as it should be; that is, that it falls short of the ideal vision the painter had in mind. And in the second and more significant respect, it is a realization that something great has taken place which the artist did not merit. Great artists have this curious realization that they are dealing with something dangerous.[7] They have come for a moment to the porch of beauty itself, and the reaction is like that in primitive religions when touching the altar of the Infinite made one guilty.

One has only to look through classical literature, mythologies of various peoples, and primitive religions to discover how universal this guilt feeling is. The ancient Greeks were certainly not a morbid people—indeed, it is often said that they did not know the meaning of our word "sin"—yet this realization of guilt runs centrally through their dramas and gives them their profound meaning. The implication is that this guilt is inherent in mankind's situation; we are stationed below the gods, said the Greek dramatists, but we are always tending to raise ourselves to the divine position.

What is the source of guilt feeling? In the first place, we can immediately see why it is inescapable in personality, for it is inseparably connected with freedom, autonomy, and moral responsibility. "Free will," Rank aptly says, "belongs to the idea of guilt or sin as inevitably as day to night."[8] Since the individual possesses creative freedom, he or she must all the time be glimpsing new possibilities; and every new possibility brings with it not only a challenge but an element of guilt feeling. In fact, challenge—the movement toward achieving the new possibility—and guilt feeling are two aspects of the same thing. Guilt feeling inheres in every state of tension in personality. Guilt feeling is the perception of a "gap"; it is, to use a crude simile, as though one were standing over a deep cleft in a mountain with one foot on one side and one on the other.

Poets and philosophers and theologians have wrestled through the ages with the problem of explaining this curious guilt feeling in the depths of humanity's being. Some have concluded that its source lies in the gap between perfection and our imperfect state: we want to paint a perfect picture or write a perfect poem, for example; but because we are fated to an existence in the human realm where everything is imperfect, we always fall short of our goals. Other thinkers, particularly the poets, have said that this guilt feeling has its source in the conflict between the animal and the spiritual natures of man. Greek Platonic thought makes it the conflict between body and mind. Some psychotherapists locate the guilt feeling in the subject-object tension within the individual. Rank holds that it arises from moral self-consciousness, and he cites the Biblical story of the fall to prove this. When Adam ate of the "tree of the knowledge of good and evil"—which signified the birth of the human capacity to perceive the difference between right and wrong—he began to feel this conscience.

However we attempt to explain this depth of spirit, we must admit that it proves that there is some contradiction in our nature. It means that we are both of the earth and of the spirit, to use popular but inaccurate terms. It means that if we try to live only in earthy, natural terms like the animals, we become neurotic; and if we try to escape entirely into the spiritual world and deny that we have bodies we also become neurotic. This situation is what people in past ages have had in mind when they spoke of being "caught between two worlds." It is in reality not a matter of *two* worlds, but of two aspects of the same world; and this is precisely what makes the problem so complicated. For everyone must hold within himself or herself the tension between these two opposite aspects of the world—the unconditioned and the conditioned. We are not horizontal creatures entirely, nor vertical creatures; we live both horizontally and vertically.[9] And the intersecting of these two planes causes a basic tension. No wonder life cannot be a simple unity!

Out of this ultimate tension comes our awareness of spirit. At the point of intersection between the vertical and horizontal arises the sense of the moral commands which Kant and many other thinkers have emphasized. At this point we also get our conception of perfection: behind or implied in the imperfect beauty of a particular tree or painting, for example, we can glimpse the form of perfect beauty.

The contradiction, thus, is proof of the presence of spirit in human nature. As we know ourselves existentially conditioned, finite, imperfect; but we are essentially bearers of spirit, and this relationship brings in the elements of the unconditioned, we are the infinite and perfect. In the light of such a tension, it is perfectly understandable that we should experience spirit at every moment.

So spirit, far from being something morbid for which we are to be ashamed, is actually a proof of our great possibilities and destiny. We should rejoice in it, for it means that a "spark disturbs our clod." More highly developed personalities feel this sense of spirit more keenly than the average, and utilize it in their further development.

Therefore, any picture of personality which leaves out the

aspect of spiritual tension is incomplete. Purely naturalistic psy-
chotherapies will always be inadequate. We can conclude that
the healthy individual must have a creative adjustment to the
Ultimate, and that a sound sense of spirit is indispensable to personality health.

From the fourth principle of personality, spiritual tension,
this guide for counseling is derived: *It is the counselor's function, while aiding the counselee to free himself or herself from
morbid guilt feeling, to assist the counselee courageously to accept and affirm the spiritual tension inherent in human nature.*

III

The Source of Personality Problems

1
Case of George

GEORGE B. MADE an excellent impression upon me when he came into my office. He must have been over six feet in height, and his physique was unusually well proportioned and handsome. He shook my hand warmly, though a little too violently, and looked at me fixedly as he spoke in a slow, carefully controlled voice.

His problem was a general unhappiness in college life. This was surprising because, to all superficial appearances, George was

41

the type who fits into campus life with eminent success. Now
a sophomore, he was considering dropping out of college altogether. Concentration on his studies had become increasingly
difficult for him during the past weeks, and a general nervousness
had come upon him for some reason he could not understand.
He had shifted his course from physical education to liberal arts,
but this had not helped. The reason for this shift, George said,
was the low morale of the faculty of the former department; he
mentioned with particular disgust the coach's drinking on one
of the trips of the minor team to which he belonged. In fact,
George condemned the whole faculty, and he had written a paper
to prove their inadequacy.

As counselor I permitted him, of course, to continue talking. He proceeded to explain to me his dissatisfaction also with
the religious work on the campus; it lacked "punch" to use his
term. He expressed a desire to get into the student religious work
and reform it—and at this moment his voice, which had previously
been calm and controlled, quivered with emotion. He was, it
became evident, a very religious individual in the ordinary sense
of the term.

I inquired about his friendships—an area which is always
significant in personality maladjustments. George answered that
he felt lonely on the campus. He did not like his roommate, a
freshman who irritated him in all sorts of small ways, such as taking
a long time getting ready for bed. George vowed he would get
him over this vexatious habit if he had to punch him every night!
In the area of relationships with the opposite sex, it came out
that George was then dating one of the more attractive and
popular young women on the campus; but he felt that she was
too frivolous and needed to be reformed into taking a greater
interest in serious things. One of the best fraternities had invited
him to become a member, a matter he was considering at the
time of these interviews. His scholastic average in college was
mediocre, although, he claimed, he forced himself to study very
hard.

This young man was clearly approaching a crisis in his personality development. During that very month his condition was

growing worse. The tensions within his personality were becoming so great and troublesome that concentration on his studies was almost impossible, and he was finding difficulty in sleeping at night. His moods changed violently from exaltation—during which he would greet me with an indomitable smile and assured me buoyantly, "I'm on top of the world today!"—to deep depression, when I sometimes observed him wandering around the campus in a sort of daze. His physical condition became so poor that he was advised by college health officials to drop out of school for a complete rest, advice which he fortunately did not take.

Here we have a condition which verges on what is commonly termed a "nervous breakdown." Many of the items cited in the above description of George's case sound like trifles, but they are symptomatic of something more serious occurring underneath. He could have become definitely neurotic if he had kept on in the path he was pursuing; the embryonic form of neurosis, indeed, is observable in this bare outline.

How shall we deal with such personality difficulties? This general condition is not infrequently found on college campuses, it will be admitted, or in any group of young people, or even older people for that matter. Shall we send George home for a rest? This would accomplish no permanent good. When he returned to some field of active life, the journey toward neurosis would be begun all over again, as the real causes in the form of unresolved personality tensions would still be present. Should the counselor try calmly to reason the matter out, trying to persuade George that the college is not as bad as he thinks and that everything can't be altogether out of joint? This would lead to an argument the result of which would only be to reinforce George's prejudices. No, the counselor must take the deeper approach of psychological understanding in order to help in such a case.

In endeavoring to understand George's personality pattern—and this is where the source of his difficulties is to be found—I learned that he was the second child following a daughter in a farming family in which considerable emphasis had been placed upon religious and ethical matters. His sister had attended this college before him and had set a fairly high record in campus achievement.

The outstanding feature observable in George's personality is his tremendous ambition. This takes the form of a strong drive to dominate others, such as his roommate, his girl, and even the college faculty. This ambition is understandable partly in connection with his excellent physique, which must have lent him much prestige in his precollege years. It is also partly understandable (but here we must go cautiously) in his relation to his older sister; second children often manifest an exaggerated ambition because of their early striving to keep up with or overtake the older child. This is particularly true of a boy following a girl, as the girl develops more rapidly in the early years.

An exaggerated ambition such as in George's drive to dominate others is often connected fundamentally with an inferiority feeling. The individual feels deeply inferior, and therefore strives to become superior by endeavoring to reform others and forcing them to conform to his or her standards. There are clear indications of George's having a strong inferiority feeling. We should expect him to express his urge to surpass others on the college athletic field, for physical education has been his main interest; but he had not succeeded in making any of the major college teams. He does not blame the coaches outright for this failure—the psychological processes are more subtle than that; he shifts the contest to the moral realm and proceeds to criticize the coaches for their beer drinking.

This young man, unusually ambitious to begin with, demands much prestige but does not succeed in achieving it in the usual channels. But he can achieve it in the moral area, and so George proceeds to center his attention upon the faults of people around him. He criticizes the college faculty and sets out to reform everything from his girl to the campus religious program. This is his way of "putting his ego on top," as Adler would say. George is very religious; but he is using his religion, as it is not uncommonly used, as an ego weapon rather than as a cause for unselfish devotion. Temporarily, this little strategy succeeds; there is no denying that in his reforming zeal, George's ego ascends on its own scale of prestige. But the victory is poorly won. His little successes in dominating will make him more antisocial, separate him the more from his group (such as his fellow students, the coaches, and his girl). And so what remnants of genuine prestige he now enjoys will steadily diminish; his inferiority feeling and basic insecurity will increase; he will need to strive the more desperately to dominate others; and his whole problem will steadily become worse.

This is the vicious circle in which persons with severe personality problems become caught. No wonder George feels nervously tense and cannot sleep or concentrate! No wonder he must exert the special control over himself manifested in his slow actions and his very steady, self-conscious manner of speaking. The tension within his personality between inferiority feeling and exaggerated ambition would, of course, make impossible for him any happy and creative living.

It is such internal tensions that cause nervous breakdowns, not simply overwork. George is caught in the vicious circle of egocentric ambition, and his personality difficulty will become steadily worse—unless a "clarification," a clearing up of wrong attitudes, occurs—until he breaks in definite neurosis. His girlfriend, we can predict, will throw him over; to the extent that she has a normal and wholesome attitude toward life, she will not brook his reforming tendencies. We can also predict that he will not join the fraternity, as to do so would be to surrender the privilege of dominating people around him.

In our counseling periods, I gradually pointed out to George these aspects of his personality pattern. At first he could not understand his selfish ambition or his urge to dominate others; he insisted he "loved" all people, and wished to reform them for their own good. We cannot expect such an individual, incidentally, to understand immediately the egocentric nature of his or her little strategies; the person who understands will have to give up his or her egocentricity, and that is the last thing in the world he or she wishes to do.

In the meantime, he was suffering; and through relating these sufferings to the mistakes in his personality pattern, we were able to turn the vicious circle of his battle for false prestige into a constructive circle.* He then began to find socially constructive means of expression for his ambition. He became a member of the campus Christian Association cabinet, but his zeal to change everything at first made it difficult for the other students to work with him. Having rejected the invitation to join the fraternity, he threw himself into a project for investigating and reforming the fraternities—this was his way of making contact with them without joining. He then organized a house group of his own, but threatened to back out at the last minute when he did not get his way in the choice of a house.

As he began to get social recognition for constructive accomplishments, however, he was gradually relieved of the intense pressure of his inferiority feeling. And consequently he did not feel so compelled to dominate. Once started on the constructive circle, George began to develop into as positive and helpful a force in his community as he had previously been negative. Without going into the details in his personality change, may we point out that it was not, of course, a simple and easy matter. The readjustment of tensions within his personality—what we term clarification—was not accomplished overnight or even in a couple of months. The readjustment brought with it its pain, the throes of rebirth from egocentricity to the socially constructive attitude toward life. But nature throws its assisting forces behind the individual once he or she has begun the constructive circle; there is a geometric progression in the respect that the more healthy the personality becomes, the more it is enabled to obtain new health. This was so for George. As soon as he gave the campus a chance, it quickly recognized his creative abilities, his physical attractiveness and his unusual energies. The very powers which had led him to the brink of neurosis now worked to increase his genuine leadership and prestige. The relationship with his girl could not be salvaged; she broke off with him, but

---

*It is to be noted that the suffering of the counselee is on the side of the overcoming of his or her problems. This means that we as counselors should use reassurance sparingly. The anxiety of the counselee is the counselor's best friend.

although he suffered greatly, he did not slip back into his old moralistic isolation.

In the spring of the year, he was elected president of the college Christian Association, a position at which he worked hard but still unsteadily and temperamentally. But by the next year his efforts had grown so socially constructive that he became prominent in the Men's League and was eventually elected to the Student Council as one of the outstanding student leaders on the campus.

2
Creative Tension

What, then, is the source of personality difficulties? If George B. in this case had been sent home in a state of nervous collapse, people would have blamed his trouble on "overwork." But we have observed through our psychological understanding of George's personality that the real reason for his breakdown would not have been too much work, but rather destructive tensions within his personality. The custom of explaining nervous breakdowns with an apologetic, "He carries so much responsibility," or "He tries to do too much," with the conclusion that all the individual needs is a good rest, is in most cases false. The more pertinent question is, why does he take on too much work? What tensions are there within his personality which will not permit him to carry the work which he has assumed? It is evident that persons often throw themselves into a great bulk of work as an escape from unsolved personality problems.

The source of personality problems is a *lack of adjustment of tensions within the personality*. In George's case, we observed a too egocentric ambition (manifesting itself in his striving to dominate) on one hand, and a too weak social interest (evidencing itself in a failure to cooperate with other people) on the other. The more unbalanced these tensions became in George's personality, the closer he would come to a nervous breakdown; the greater this lack of adjustment, in other words, the more neurotic he would grow. Only when the tensions were adjusted into some kind of functional accord would George be able to express himself creatively and effectively in the outside world and thus achieve the genuine prestige he craved.

Each of us has experienced this process of adjustment of tensions within his own personality. It is something dynamic, creative, going on at all times. A man walks down the street, for example; and in talking to the first person he accosts he experiences a readjusting of the tensions between his desire to dominate and his interest in the other as a fellow human being. Or he comes home and reads a book, and every idea that catches his attention sets his personality tensions into a new adjustment. Every time one experiences a feeling that one "ought" to do this or that, or a feeling of inferiority, or of triumph or despair, one's personality tensions are being readjusted.

Thus personality is never static. It is alive, ever changing, mobile; it is plastic, variable, almost protean. We should not therefore speak of "balance" in personality, or "equilibrium," for these imply that one's personality tensions can be set once for all. Becoming static is in this realm synonymous with death. Life is not like tuning a radio and leaving it there; it is rather like continually tuning it to a varying wavelength, namely, the new experiences of each day which, flowing out of the infinite creativity of life, are always fresh and different.

At the same time, this does not mean that one is an altogether different person from what one was yesterday, or that the individual is blown hither and yon like a wisp in the wind. There is a certain continuity because of the tendencies in the unconsciousness of the individual which reach deep down into past experience. What the person was a month ago, or a year or five or many years ago, leaves a certain psychic force within the unconsciousness which affects the person's tensions today. But these tendencies surging up from unconsciousness are also mobile and dynamic; one has an infinite number of them available at any given instance. That is why even habits cannot be static. It is doubtful whether there is any such thing as a real habit in healthy living, as there is no situation that does not bring in a new element of experience which affects the tensions within one's personality. Life is much more creative, much more variable and pregnant with possibilities than most people realize.

We use the word "tension" advisedly. For there is always a certain stretching, even a stress and strain in one's personality. There is a pull, for example, between where one is now and where one must be in an hour, and this awareness of obligation to be some other place exerts a certain tension in the mind. There is a tension between the work one did yesterday and the work one is to do tomorrow, and one carries this strain along from day to day as though bearing the burden of labor upon one's back. The great tension, of course, is that which we speak of broadly as the tension between what one is and what one feels one ought to be. Personality is like a web, to venture a very imperfect simile; for it consists of lines of tension between an infinitely larger number of points, the tensions and the points of attachment being continually subject to change.

It is a serious mistake, therefore, to speak of personality without tensions—to imply, for example, that the healthy mental condition is a blissful absence of tensions. To be sure, tensions which are seriously maladjusted and are therefore stretched to the breaking point do result in mental breakdown. But the thing desired is *adjustment* of tensions, not escaping them. One could not get rid of personality tensions even if one wanted to; the neurotic attempts it, by such schemes, for example, as remaining indoors and never meeting other people, but the result is stagnation and ultimate breakdown. One must courageously accept the necessity for tensions and then work out the most effective adjustment so that one's personality will express itself most creatively in the outside world.

The point deserves emphasis that the locus of the personality problem is the adjustment of tensions *within* the individual. Outside factors play a role, of course; but their importance lies in the fact that the personality draws them into itself and uses them as pivot points. The talk about the need for "adjustment to environment,'' which was so common in the dilettantes of the new psychology several years ago, implies that one's main concern should be making oneself over to fit one's environment. But this falsifies the problem and belittles human personality. As though a person were a piece of rubber useful only because it can be stretched to fit anything! Yes, adjustment is necessary, but not merely to something outside the individual. It is a creative, dynamic, primarily inner process.

The counselor should guard against the counselee's tendency to shift the problem to some area outside himself or herself, blaming, for example, someone in his environment. It was a wise young woman who once came to me with the statement, ''I can't get along with my family; tell me what is wrong with me.'' It is most fruitful for the counselor, though taking duly into consideration all environmental factors, to push the difficulty back to the tensions *within* the personality of the counselee.

Even so apparently objective a factor as sex expression becomes important to personality because of the inward tensions it sets up. If it were only a question of man's expressing the sex urge in reality, expression equaling mental health and nonexpression equaling neurosis, what a simple problem it would be! But sex causes personality difficulties, not to the extent that it is objectively expressed in reality, but according to how the individual takes this expression or lack of it. One of my counselees had previously gone to a professor to talk over his problem of general unhappiness and melancholy, and had been advised by the professor to go out and express himself sexually. The student experimented in the field but found that it made his difficulty all the worse. All attempts to work out the problem entirely *outside one's self* can make the individual just as neurotic as ascetic repression. Freud makes it clear that the problem of sex is one of the adjusting of tensions within the personality—the tension of the sex urge, the social requirements as they appear to the individual, and the influence of moral training, all forming a none too simple situation. What is desired is a clarification of attitudes, and right behavior results from this.

Something outside the individual is used, generally, as an occasion for the personality breakdown, such as a love affair, or a severe examination, or the death of a member of the family. Here is John Doe, let us say, who commits suicide when his sweetheart throws him over. People say, "If only he had never met the woman, this would not have happened." Possibly—but probably not. He carried neurotic behavior potentially within himself, and it would have come out in some form sooner or later. The significant area in regard to these tensions is within the personality, although the individual will be continually acting and reacting in the environment, using elements in it as pivotal points. George B., we remember, was angry at his roommate, but the roommate in the case was merely the most convenient pivotal point for his irritability; and we can be sure if the roommate had not been around George would have used somebody else as a butt for his irritability. The personality uses the points in the environment as nails on which to attach the end threads of tension. *Thus these outside elements become important because they are related to the personality tensions within*. The personality, we may say, takes these elements of the environment into itself and uses them in its own structure.

The tendency to blame heredity or environment for personality difficulties should be avoided. The unattractive woman may say, "Well, I just wasn't born beautiful"; but the counselor can often indicate to her that her so-called unattractiveness is due to mistaken attitudes and therefore wrong use of the physical form with which she was born. Neuroses—the general classification of personality difficulties when they become severe—are not inherited but are wrong ways of using what one inherits.

Environment is extremely important as the arena in which the individual struggles for adjustment, but to regard environment as causal is neither fruitful nor accurate. Environment furnishes the chessboard, and, in fact, most of the pawns with which the game is played; given the board and pawns, however, one cannot predict *how* the game will be played.

It is not within the scope of this book to delve into the very important question of the bearing of social conditions upon the individual's personality problems. Such diseases of society as unemployment, economic insecurity of all sorts, fear of war and the social upheaval that follows war have a tremendous bearing upon the adjustment of individuals involved. Spasmodic unemployment with its consequent continuous burden of insecurity increases the personality tensions with a severity the importance of which cannot be exaggerated. It is a truism to say that mental health and a healthy social order are intimately interdependent.

Granting all this and more, it is still true, however, that the personality difficulty itself is a matter of adjustment of tensions within the individual; and the endeavor to locate it outside is to miss the point of the matter. To be sure, unfavorable environments such as that of the child growing up in the slums make personality problems more likely. But it is a commonplace that two children growing up in poverty-stricken conditions may develop very differently. In fact, two children in the same home, thus beginning with almost identical heredity and almost identical environment, not only may, but, as we discover, *will*, develop into appreciably different types of personality. Heredity and environment set limits within which the individual does his developing; he who comes from a line of short ancestors need not expect to grow extraordinarily tall—but his physical health does not depend upon how tall he is. Personality health is a *qualitative* not a quantitative matter.

The mere changing of environment, although sometimes helpful, is not the essential need. A daughter away at college, for example, becomes involved in an unfortunate love affair, and the parents remove her to another school. This may help temporarily, but the probability is that the young woman will get into similar difficulties again unless some better adjustment of her personality has occurred in the meantime. *"They change their skies but not their minds*, who fly across the seas," writes Horace and personality problems are a question *of changing one's mind*.

As counselors we sometimes seek to effect a change in certain features of the environments of our counselees, particularly if they are children. In counseling with adults, counselors will not suggest outright a change in the environment even though it appears advisable; they will rather aid the individuals to understand themselves in relation to the environment, and then the decision to change will come from the counselees themselves. The changing of the vocational factor in the environment often comes into the picture: a person of a peculiarly artistic temperament will occasionally be caught in an occupation which makes the overcoming of the neurosis almost humanly impossible. It is within the counselor's province to assist individuals to discover their right vocations; but this kind of guidance, it should be remembered, is one degree removed from direct dealing with personality problems. Even beyond this there will be the times when the counselor gives the individual specific help in finding a job; to one burdened with economic insecurity practical aid is at the moment more important than psychological understanding. But in these instances the counselor, strictly speaking, is dealing only indirectly with personality difficulties. When dealing with the personality problem itself, the counselor does not permit the counselee to shift the responsibility to the environment, but aids the counselee to accept responsibility for the future and helps the counselee to use the environment in the most creative way.

A young woman once came to me for counseling who had lived through the most unfavorable of environments. She had grown up in a stepmother's house with two step-aunts, a step-brother and several other in-laws and grandparents, who had crowded her even out of her own bed. There had been continual quarreling in the house; and the adults naturally picked her, the stepchild, as a convenient butt for the expression of their rancor. One who thinks that environment makes the person would expect this young woman to be, after fifteen years of family torment, a cynical, suspicious, scheming misanthrope. But, as a matter of fact, she was an attractive, socially minded young woman, possessing more humor and gaiety than her peers. She had met her unhappy situation by developing a more than usual amount of humor and buoyancy. We could cite many similar cases where the individual has used an unfavorable environment as a ladder to climb to an unusually effective personality adjustment. Bad environment increases the possibility of neurosis, but the individual may use this very potentiality for a more creative adjustment to living. To assist in the accomplishment of this is the function of the counselor.

3
Structure of Our Difficulties

Let us now get more clearly in mind the structure of personality difficulties. The lack of adjustment of the personality may manifest itself in all sorts of symptoms, such as embarrassment, timidity, extraordinary shyness, continuous worry and anxiety, fears of meeting people, special fear of failure in one's job, and inability to concentrate. Embarrassment, for example, is a sign that the tensions within the personality block each other, like two wrestlers who have such strong holds on each other that neither can move. Consequently, the individual cannot speak or think freely and cannot express himself or herself effectively in the outside world. Such persons consequently may be severely handicapped in the execution of their work, or unable to make normal social contacts and thus solve their love and marriage problems or in other ways fail to develop and utilize their potentialities.

Persons with such personality difficulties have a conflict within themselves which to some extent paralyzes them. They are, as the expression goes, at odds with themselves. Because they are at odds with themselves, they are also at odds with their social group. The two are conflicts on two flanks of the same battle. George B. could not get along with the other students because he insisted on reforming them, but this was in turn connected with his inner drive to dominate. Attaining mental health meant in his case, as it does in most such cases, a simultaneous adjustment of the tensions within himself and the adjustment of his relations with his fellows.

Adler makes the social adjustment the criterion, the "fruit," by which the personality clarification is judged. But this runs the danger of glorifying superficial adjustment to society. Actually, behavior toward others results from attitudes; and there is only one seat of attitudes—namely, the mind of the individual in question. Persons who have made their adjustment to society without clarification of their attitudes, that is, at the price of hypocrisy, have made no adjustment at all, and their little structures will collapse. Likewise, it is possible for an individual, such as Socrates or St. Francis or Mother Teresa, to have attained a creative adjustment of inner personality tensions and be for that very reason out of harmony with the imperfect society in which the person lives.

When a personality problem becomes so severe that individuals cannot carry on in their work or their relations with other people, we describe it by the term "neurosis." A student, for example, had the relatively common problem of studying in a state of highly nervous tension before examinations. This grew more severe until she became sick the night before an examination and was excused, and she then developed the convenient neurotic scheme of falling sick before *all* examinations. A similar neurotic condition may be brought on by a severe emotional conflict which cannot be resolved by the individual.

The term "neurosis" springs from the root word "nerves," because mental disorders were first observed through the nervousness they generated in the form of anxiety, worry, or even actual trembling of parts of the body. But the term does not imply that anything is wrong with the nerves organically; it refers, rather, to a personality state. "Psychosis" is the term for that state of mental disorder more severe than neurosis, which includes those many forms of mental disease popularly lumped together as insanity. Some psychoses are organic, such as those caused by disease attacking the tissues of the nervous system, but many are functional. The counselor does not, of course, attempt to deal with such conditions, and the particular value in being able to recognize psychotic conditions is that he or she can refer the individual to professional psychiatric care.*

Neuroses are functional in root, that is, they are attributable to forms of behavior and mental attitudes rather than organic

---

*Of course, all kinds of persons will come to most counselors, and some will be on the verge of a psychotic break. The important counsel to the counselor is not to get too upset when the person seems to be going into a psychosis. It is, to be sure, a difficult thing to listen to another person who is at the edge of such an episode. As counselors, our function in such situations is to keep the discussion as much as possible on the realistic level. Then, after the session, one can refer the person to some psychiatric facility which is prepared to deal with him or her.

disorders. There may be concomitant organic factors, as Adler has demonstrated, in a neurosis. Many organic states are results of neurotic states of mind, such as low blood pressure or, to cite the classical illustration, blindness coming with shellshock during war. The counselor should be aware of the physical condition of the counselee so as to bring into the picture all the relevant organic factors, either causal or resultant, and can often get aid in this through consultation with the family doctor of the counselee, or the college health officials in campus situations. The counselor's concern is the functional aspect of the difficulty, namely, making healthy the attitudes and behavior patterns of the individual.

It is generally recognized in modern psychotherapy that there is no hard and fast line between so-called "normal" people and neurotics, or between neurotics and psychotics. Many types of psychotics are required by law to be confined to institutions for the insane; but psychiatrists and judges admit that the decision as to whom to adjudge insane and whom to dismiss as merely "a little off" is at times unavoidably arbitrary. It is possible for an individual to progress from a simple personality problem to neurosis and from neurosis to psychosis, and then back again. One could cite many cases similar to that of Mrs. D., who had had personality difficulties in her youth but had moved with a fair degree of success through grade school and high school. Her personality conflicts became more pronounced in college, and we should then have classified her as neurotic. Several years later, in the course of an emotional and physical strain, she suddenly developed into schizophrenia and had to be confined to a mental hospital. She is now out of the hospital, living in fairly healthy fashion, and is to all appearances as "normal" as people around her.

Everyone has personality problems, and everyone is continuously in the process of readjusting the tensions within his or her personality. No one is completely "normal." For example, we all have had the wish at some time not to meet a certain other person; we may have crossed the street, though we were probably ashamed of it afterward, to avoid encountering this person. Now if this grows into a desire to avoid a number of persons, or possibly everybody, so that we remain always behind closed doors at home, we shall have regressed into the neurotic state. In each of us there is the urge to dominate that drove George B. to the brink of severe neurosis. The difference is that those of us who are called "normal" have this tendency better adjusted in the constellation of our personality tensions. To speak frankly, I have never dealt with a counselee in whose difficulty I did not see myself, at least potentially. Every counselor, theoretically, will have this same experience. It is a matter of "There, but for the grace of God, go I." There is no room for arrogance or self-righteousness, but all the room in the world for humility, in the counseling occupation.

It is only wise for each of us to become acquainted with his or her little neurotic tendencies, even if they be no more severe than the common practice of running other people down in gossip or taking a drink of liquor to brace one's self for an important occasion. As Adler puts it, "Minor difficulties equal normality; major difficulties equal neurosis." Or, phrased probably more accurately, emotional conflicts which can be managed equal normality; those conflicts which one cannot manage equal neurosis. If one recognizes one's special neurotic tendencies, one is more able to guard against their throwing the personality into definite disorder at some time of emotional crisis.

We have used the word "normal" in quotation marks, as it is an ideal rather than a reality. The norm is a standard drawn from our knowledge of the possibilities in a situation; it is partly based upon the range of expectation, but, like physical health, it is not a limiting category. It is possible to measure what is wrong or unhealthy in personality, as the neurosis leads the sick person into all kinds of errors, but we cannot measure "rightness" in this area. We can only free the individual to develop according to his or her own unique form. Thus, being normal does not at all mean becoming static or "average" or fitted into the same pigeonhole with everyone else; it means just the opposite. The norm for personality is in a sense the ideal; and it is based upon principles of creativity, such as freedom, individuality, and others which shall be discussed in the next chapter.

The possibility of readjusting personality tensions is nature's greatest gift to humanity. It means growth, development, fulfilling of one's potentialities. Readjustment of personality tensions is synonymous with creativity. The especially creative person is precisely one whose personality tensions are especially susceptible to adjustment; he or she is more sensitive and suffers more but enjoys greater possibilities. The neurotic individual is one who has the special possibility of readjusting personality tensions, who is required by the situation, in fact, to do so, but who because of fear refuses and attempts to freeze into static training formulas. Once such persons take courage and begin the process of readjustment, they may suddenly become unusually creative individuals. It is not an accident that the persons who are most sensitive to others, who may most dread meeting other people, are often precisely those who, when they turn this sensitivity into constructive channels, become most likable and effective in personal relationships.

One has only to glance through history to see that the most creative individuals are often the most obviously neurotic. Van Gogh was neurotic during most of his life and held off psychosis only by means of his tremendous creativity, by which he was able to adjust the terrific tensions in his personality. He existed on the thin, knife-blade edge of sanity only with difficulty, and this is connected with the creativity that made him a great artist. The great artists have greater neurotic potentialities. Like Dostoevski and Nietzsche, they appear to fluctuate between more or less neurotic conditions. The more sensitive the inward balance of tensions, the greater the creativity. This is not to glorify neurosis; nor is it to say, with the title of a book, "be glad you're neurotic," but it is to say that neurotic tendencies, if confronted courageously and constructively, do mean possibilities for special creative development.

Each of us, then, can achieve a better adjustment of our personality tensions. No one has "arrived." The difference between the neurotic who can barely keep a job and the "average" individual who does passably well is certainly no greater than that between this average person and the one who has become so clarified in his or her personality that he or she is able to take advantage of all creative possibilities and move rapidly up to increasingly influential and effective positions.

The helping of these so-called "normal" people to a more creative adjustment is the work of the counselor. The counselor not only helps individuals below the average to come up to it, but, even more important, aims to assist those who appear to be average to take advantage of their unique possibilities and grow up in richer development. The following case may illustrate this.

When this young man, whom we may call John C., came to college, he passed as a typical freshman, possibly a little above average. During his freshman year, he appeared unusually shy; he blushed often and at committee meetings sat stiffly and soberly.

In his sophomore year, he came to me with the request for a "psychological analysis." Though the process of counseling should scarcely be called that, we did arrange for a series of consultations. In the course of the counseling, it came out that he had been brought up by a grandmother, and though he had been rather successful in his small high school as student council member and editor of the annual, he had always lived in rather solitary fashion. He could not remember playing much as a child, but he did remember mowing the lawn regularly and doing his little chores by himself.

He was even then writing poems to "death." John C., evidently, was the type we customarily term "introvert." He had no satisfactory friendships with girls because of his shyness, which took the form of pronounced soberness when he was in social groups. He was distinctly intelligent, although his thought and speech moved slowly; his main interests were philosophy, religion, and the "heavier" forms of literature.

So we see John C., a fairly normal person but tending on the whole to withdraw from life. He might have become a rather good teacher; he probably never would have become so neurotic as to be confined to a mental hospital. But his personality was full of little inhibitions, and he certainly had not become freed to develop his creative powers to anything like their full possibility. Like the great majority of people, he would have pushed along through

life carrying such an internal burden of inhibitions and petty conflicts that he would have ended up merely "John C., a little above
average."

A year after our consultations, I received a letter from him
saying,

> I've had a swell time in school this last year; better than dur-
> ing any other year. Do you remember the series of talks we had
> a year ago relative to my outlook on life? Well, they've made a
> huge difference in me this year, in more ways than one; and
> though I still have my Blue Mondays, I think I've taken some
> long strides in overcoming the deep-set egocentricity which was
> my great nemesis a year ago. I've dropped many of my prejudices
> and fears: I've crawled quite a way out of my shell. Even Hank,
> who has been my roommate this year, has more than once re-
> marked the general change he has noticed in me. And I am find-
> ing this matter of "putting away childish things" a hell of a lot
> of fun.

When I next met him he had been elected president of an
important student organization and was in New York attending
an intercollegiate conference and meeting influential people with
zest and enjoyment. He appeared to have been "freed,"; and
his personality, like all freed personalities, was developing by
geometric progression.

IV   *Empathy—Key To The Counseling Process*

Having DISCUSSED THE nature of personality, we are now confronted by the subsequent question of how personality functions. How does one personality meet and react to another? The answer lies in the concept of *empathy*, the general term for the contact, influence, and interaction of personalities.

"Empathy" comes to us as a translation of the word of the German psychologists, "einfulung," which means literally "feeling into." It is derived from the Greek "pathos," meaning a deep and strong feeling akin to suffering, prefixed with the preposition "in." The parallel with the word "sympathy" is obvious. But whereas sympathy denotes "feeling with" and may lead into sentimentality, empathy means a much deeper state of identification of personalities in which one person so feels into the other as temporarily to lose his or her own identity. It is in this profound and somewhat mysterious process of empathy that understanding, influence, and the other significant relations between persons take place. Thus, in discussing empathy we are considering not only the key process in counseling, but also the key to practically all of the work of teachers, preachers, and others whose vocation depends upon influencing people.

To begin with an example, let me describe the case of a certain student who came into my office for a counseling interview. He approached rather timidly, shaking my hand with a clammy palm and smiling apologetically. Though large in stature, he gave the impression of a big child, and as he spoke he blushed continually and gazed down at the floor. Soon he was relating in a low, hesitating voice certain occurrences in his childhood and other aspects of his home background that lay behind his present perplexities.

While he talked I sat perfectly relaxed and let my eyes rest on his face. I permitted myself to become absorbed in his story; and soon I was so completely engrossed that I was unconscious of our physical surroundings and aware only of this boy's frightened eyes, his tremulous voice, and the fascinating human drama he was describing.

He told how his father had beaten him during his boyhood on the farm, and how he had grown up without parental love or understanding. During this moment, I felt the pain of his father's beatings, curious as it may seem, as though I myself were receiving the blows. Then he told of running away to high school, where he had supported himself alone under great handicaps. Through high school he had been burdened by an overpowering sense of inferiority. And as he described this inferiority feeling, a depression occurred in myself as though the inferiority had been my own.

Then the young man spoke of his early wish to attend college, which had been met by his parents' sarcastic prediction that he would not be able to last a semester. With bulldog determination, he had nevertheless arrived on the campus, practically penniless. Since then—he was now a sophomore—he had been working his way while struggling to keep up in studies for which he was poorly prepared. Speaking then of his college experience, he described the shyness and feelings of inferiority which continued to oppress him and the loneliness that he suffered even in the midst of campus life.

The point to be observed in this illustration is that the psychic states of the counselee and the counselor were to some extent identified. As counselor I had become so absorbed in his story that his emotions had become my emotions. His feelings of desperation as he struggled through high school, his realization of the loneliness of existence and the harshness of destiny, became my own experiences, felt on my pulse as they had originally been on his. And when he concluded by stating his determination to stick it out at college if it killed him, I felt a certain excitement as though this resolution had been made by my own will.

This partial identification was so real that if I had spoken aloud, my voice would no doubt have partaken of the hesitant, quavering quality of his. The conclusion is forced upon us that the ego or psychic state of the counselor had temporarily become merged with that of the counselee; he and I were one psychic unity.

This is empathy. It is the feeling, or the thinking, of one personality into another until some state of identification is achieved. In this identification real understanding between people can take place; without it, in fact, no understanding is possible. It is clear that the experience of empathy comes into every counselor's day dozens of times, whether it is recognized as such or not. Empathy is not a magical process even though it is mysterious. It appears difficult to understand precisely because it is so common and basic. As Adler points out, this identifying of one's self with the other person takes place to some extent in every conversation. It is the fundamental process in love. Most persons have never taken the trouble to analyze their capacity to empathize, and consequently they possess the ability only in rudimentary and undeveloped form. But ministers and teachers and others who deal intimately with persons had best endeavor to understand it, as their success depends upon their ability to accomplish this walking with another person into the deepest chambers of his soul.

Empathy is experienced, in the first place, with inanimate objects. The bowler sways in the direction he or she wishes the ball to roll as though to influence it with his or her own body called "body English." Whole grandstands of people will heave with a football team, everyone bracing and grunting as though each was making the tackle!

1
Empathy in Art

In artistic experience empathy is also basic, as the individual must in some way identify with the object if it is to be experienced aesthetically. Thus people speak of music "carrying them away," or of the violin playing upon the strings of their emotions, or of the changing colors of the sunset creating a corresponding change in their emotions. Jung makes empathy the center of his theory of aesthetics. The person looking at the artistic object "becomes the object; he identifies himself with it, and in this way gets rid of himself."[1] This is the secret of the cathartic power of art—the aesthetic experience does actually take the artist or the spectator out of himself or herself. Aristotle has classically described how seeing a great dramatic tragedy purges the soul of the observer, precisely for the reason that the tragedy is enacted on the stage of the observer's own soul while watching it on the real stage. Drama is the form of art in which empathy is most easily understood; for there occurs the very obvious identification of the actors with the fictitious characters they are representing, as well as the more subtle identification of the observers with the actors.

This cathartic quality, resulting from empathy, is present in good conversation. We even might, in fact, judge the merit of a particular conversation by asking how much it has taken us out of ourselves. Counseling has the cathartic function superlatively. The counselor has to go out of himself or herself almost completely; that is why a period of genuine and intense counseling will leave the counselor curiously freed from his or her own problems. At the same time, the counselor will feel strangely fatigued, just as the artist is fatigued after two hours of painting.

Adler recognizes empathy as one of the creative functions in personality and goes on to say:

> Empathy occurs in the moment one human being speaks with another. It is impossible to understand another individual if it is impossible at the same time to identify one's self with him. . . . If we seek for the origin of this ability to act and feel as if we were someone else, we can find it in the existence of an inborn social feeling. This is, as a matter of fact, a cosmic feeling and a reflection of the connectedness of the whole cosmos which lives in us; it is an inescapable characteristic of being a human being.[2]

One principle in the matter of establishing rapport concerns the *ability to use the other person's langauge*. Language is the ordinary channel of empathy, and two persons who have progressed to some degree of personal identification will find themselves automatically employing a common mode of speech. In fact, one could measure the degree of empathy of the minister with the congregation or the teacher with students by their ability to speak the others' language. While living among various peoples in Europe, I observed that when the other person, say my French companion, spoke in English to facilitate my understanding, I found my empathy only slight. The person was, so to speak, coming to me. But when I translated myself into Greek to converse with peasants in the villages of Greece, I experienced a pronounced empathy with them. The conclusion is that one can best identify with another by using the language of the other.

Jung describes the *merging* process here involved, both the counselor and the counselee being changed: "The meeting of two personalities is like the contact of two chemical substances;

if there is any reaction, both are transformed. We should expect the doctor to have an influence on the patient in every effective psychic treatment; but this influence can only take place when he, too, is affected by the patient."[3]

The original source of the capacity for empathy is found, so far as we can determine, in the ability of primitive peoples to identify themselves with each other and with their community and totem. This is termed "*participation mystique.*" Levy-Bruhl, the great French anthropologist who has pursued this subject with particular depth, says that the primitive people identify themselves with each other in such a complete way as to produce a "community of essence" and a "*continuum* of spiritual powers." "A certain community of being is thus immediately felt, not only between members of the same totemic family, but between all entities of any kind whatsoever which form part of the same class and are linked together in mystic fellowship."[4] The child feels the effect of what its parents eat, and the hunter away in the forest is influenced by what his wife eats or does back in the village.

This may seem a far cry from our modern individuality in civilization, but as a matter of fact it is not. Our assumption that persons can isolate themselves and live their own lives is superficial and illusory; it is a result of the exaggerated attempt to be rational and apply logical separations to life. Human beings even in civilization are creatures of very collective modes of thought and behavior is proven in modern nationalistic trends. If we had earlier recognized this, we should not now be confronted with such demonic exaggerations of collective psychology as appear in the totalitarian states.

Participation in other persons or objects gives us an understanding of them which is far more intimate and meaningful than mere scientific analysis or empirical observation. For "understanding," be it of things as different as a rubber ball and a period of history, actually means this identification of subjective and objective resulting in a new condition which transcends them both. Levy-Bruhl adds that this is particularly true in the matter of our knowledge of God. Whatever content we give that term we can never arrive at an understanding of God through purely rational, logical methods; the individual must participate in God. The customary term for this method is "faith." Levy-Bruhl describes it more fully as "direct and intimate contact with the essence of being, by intuition, interpenetration, the mutual communion of subject and object, full participation and immanence, in short, that which Plotinus has described as ecstasy."[5]

To know the meaning of beauty or love or any of the so-called values of life, we must let ourselves participate in them. Thus "experiencing" them, we shall know them "on our pulse," as Keats puts it. It is sheer folly to think that another person can be known by analysis or formulas; here understanding as participation comes into its own. In other words, it is impossible to know another person without being, broadly speaking, in love with him or her. But this state means that both persons will be changed by the identification the love brings about.

Thus it is literally true that love works a change in the personalities of both the lover and the loved. It may tend to make them become more alike, or it may draw the loved one up toward the ideal in the lover's mind. Love therefore carries tremendous psychological power. It is the greatest force available in the influencing and transforming of personality.[6]

The counselor works basically through the process of empathy. Both the counselor and the counselee are taken out of themselves and become merged in a common psychic entity. The emotions and will of each become part of this new psychic entity. Consequently, the problem of the counselee is dumped on the "new person," and the counselor then bears half of it. And the psychological stability of the counselor's clarity, courage and strength of will, will carry through to the counselee, thus lending great assistance in his personality struggle.

Let it be clearly understood that empathy does not mean identifying one's experiences with the counselee, as occurs when the counselor remarks, "Yes, that happened to me too when I was such and such an age." Except in rare circumstances, there is no place in true counseling for the reminiscences of the counselor. All of this comes out of egocentricity, and empathy is precisely the opposite of egocentricity. The previous experiences of the counselor do not come into the counseling situation *as such*. Understanding the counselee according to his or her own unique pattern is the goal; and the counselor who says or thinks, "I had that problem myself and I met it in such and such a way," will be projecting himself or herself into the situation in a way which may be very vicious. The counselor's previous experience will aid immeasurably in understanding the counselee—in this regard, previous experience is indispensable; but such experience will contribute only indirectly. At the moment of the counseling situation it would be theoretically well if the counselor forgot he or she ever had any similar experiences; the counselor's function is to give himself or herself up, be almost a *tabula rasa*, surrender to the empathetic situation.

2
Mental Transference

The question arises concerning the connection between empathy and mental telepathy, or other special aspects of psychical transference. Mental telepathy denotes a transfer of ideas between persons by means beyond our known senses. It has clear affinities with the empathetic process.

Empathy is the general term for all participation of one personality in the psychic state of another, and the hypothesis of telepathy refers to one aspect of this participation. The proof of the existence of empathy does not depend on the ultimate substantiation of mental telepathy; the former occurs, as we have indicated above, in such everyday phenomena as conversation and simple human understanding. But if telepathy is scientifically demonstrated, as it may in some future time be, we shall have a very vivid and cogent illustration of one aspect of the participation of personalities in each other.

It is certainly true that much more psychical transference occurs between persons than is ordinarily admitted. All through history people have had the suspicion that transference of thought by means beyond the word and gesture was occurring even though they could not prove it. Freud remarked that this is particularly true between children and parents, in which regard a number of instances of telepathy have been, he believed, adequately substantiated.[7] The source of the telepathic processes, Freud suggested, may be a "communal" mind among persons similar to that prevailing among insects, this possibly being the archaic, original method of communication between human beings.

It would be a serious and unnecessary hindrance to our understanding of human personality if we were to close our minds to the possibility of psychical transference simply because experimental science has not yet amassed sufficient data in the field. As a matter of fact, the very hypotheses science eventually proves experimentally are often truths which were stated centuries earlier by philosophers and intuitive psychologists, such as the atomic theory.* The fruitful point of view is, we suggest, the frank admission that much communication and understanding occurs between persons by means subtler and more intangible than the word or gesture. This understanding in general is empathy; and the specific methods of communication, physical or psychical, are to be regarded as various aspects or instruments of empathy.

Much communication occurs between persons by means of little gestures of which they are not aware, by the almost imperceptible variations in the expression of the face, by faint winces at unpleasant thoughts and a slight lightening of the countenance at pleasing ideas. The facial expression, varying through an infinite number of nuances, reflects the inner thoughts for those who can read; and those activities even in the form of posture and the twitching of fingers is an expression of inner mental states. People read much more of this nonvocal expression of their fellows

---

*The atomic hypothesis was stated by Epicurus in the third century B.C. in Greece, and was revised and re-stated by Leibnitz in the eighteenth century.

than they realize. Where physical transference of thought leaves off and nonphysical begins, we are not now able to say.

May I relate an experience of my own, which will be common to most people, to illustrate another approach to our question? Often when talking to another person I have a curious suspicion that the person is reading more of my thoughts than I am telling in words. With this suspicion I experience a moment of fright. Then I ask myself, why should I be afraid he or she will know what is going on in my mind? I proceed to remind myself that I really have nothing to keep hidden; he or she may read my thoughts, and in fact I am quite willing to assist with the spoken word on any matter about which he or she may inquire.

The point to be noticed is that by this little psychological device I am able to be more honest with the other person. I am able, that is, to give up to some extent the little game of deceit all human beings play with each other most of the time. And I give up the deceit by the means, curiously enough, of a *hypothesis of mental telepathy*, assuming that the other can read my mind and that there is therefore no point in keeping anything from that person. Psychical transference thus has its ethical side in practical living. It means honesty. If people could read each other's minds, lying would be no longer possible; honesty would be not only the best but the only policy, as deception would be impossible.

The deeper one penetrates into psychological understanding, the more difficult it becomes to lie. One still tends to deceive others in such universal ways as putting one's best foot forward; but psychological insight springs up at the very moment to remind us that there really is no ultimate value in always keeping the best front up. This understanding unmasks the tendencies toward self-deceit, and it discloses the real motive behind the false rationalization which one's vanity attempts. It might conceivably be true, as some uninstructed persons seem to fear, that psychological understanding would empower vicious individuals to be more demonic and unscrupulous; as they would have learned subtler techniques of twisting others to their will. But this is mostly a bogey. On the whole it is true that understanding of depth psychology tends to remove the possibility of dishonesty and thus force one into greater honesty.

"It may cause general astonishment," wrote Freud, "to learn how much stronger is the impulse to tell the truth than is usually supposed. Perhaps it is a result of my occupation with psycho-analysis that I can scarcely lie any more."[8]

Every human being has the tendency to deceive others, because his or her ego is always striving to raise its own prestige at the expense of others. In ethical persons this does not take the form of outright lying, but rather the form of the continuous endeavor to appear something different from, usually better than, they actually are. The purist who does not recognize the tendency to deceive others is twice deceived—his or her ego has learned the game so well that it has completely deceived the person himself or herself, and therefore has an open highway through which to deceive the world. Human motives always have more or less of the ego bias, and this with its consequent tendency to deceive others must be recognized before one is in a position to move toward greater honesty. This is why "good" people who do not admit their evil tendencies may be more evil, as Jesus so often pointed out, than bad people who do recognize their failings.

Deceit of others and self-deceit go hand in hand. In fact, a person who did not deceive himself or herself to some degree could not long continue to deceive others, as he or she would recognize the folly of the trick. Both kinds of deceit may succeed temporarily, but only to fail the more disastrously in the end, precisely because they *are deceit*. The more penetrating one's insight into the deep workings of personality, the more one is convinced of the uselessness of trying to fool either one's self or others.

Let us analyze an instance of so-called harmless deceit, the notorious and common "white lie." Mrs. Brown, say, invites Mrs. DeWitt to dinner. For some reason, the latter does not wish to attend; she may send any of the stock excuses, from the death of a relative to the pressure of a previous engagement. Supposing that Mrs. DeWitt is an individual without particular understanding of human nature, she will assume that Mrs. Brown has believed her white lie, and she will let the whole matter drop.

We have a right to suppose, however, that Mrs. Brown suspects the other's deceit. We do not often hear of people's suspecting each other's deceit, because there are certain psychological reasons why the deceived individual does not wish to admit the fact. In this illustration Mrs. Brown would not publicly mention her suspicion; she would probably not even say anything about it to her husband; in fact, she might even refuse to admit it to herself. Entertaining the suspicion would mean recognizing that Mrs. DeWitt did not wish to dine at her house, and this would be an intolerable blow to her vanity. So she would suppress her suspicion into her subconscious; vanity being queen, Mrs. Brown prefers to bask in her self-deceit rather than to face the truth. This suppression might come out in the form of embarrassment at her next social dinner; in any case, it would not make for healthy personality.

The constructive approach Mrs. Brown should have taken would consist of the frank admission of her suspicions and an honest asking of herself the real reason underlying Mrs. DeWitt's wish to stay away. Then she would be in a position to turn her attention to correcting the mistakes which had created a disturbance in the relationship. Frankly recognizing the situation—though it would temporarily lower Mrs. Brown's "ego prestige"—would not necessarily result in her developing an "inferiority complex"; she could realize that all human relationships fall short of perfection and that one can best recognize this imperfection and be fitted thereby to make the relationships more nearly perfect.

Sometimes an individual is troubled by the fact that he or she tends, apparently without being able to prevent it, to think uncomplimentary things about the person with whom he or she is talking. The same process of "running the other down" is occurring on the other side, and consequently the thoughts each "reads" in the other's mind are not very palatable. Perhaps the individual will say on experiencing this, "I think so-and-so dislikes me," but more often will not mention the suspicion. It is best to admit the suspicion if one feels it, but, as a matter of fact, the mistrust is not in this case an accurate interpretation of the situation. We have here not a matter of one person "disliking" the other, but simply the juxtaposition of egos, each of which is striving for the prestige and superiority in the relationship.

It is very difficult for the ego to accept a position of inferiority. A person who actually does feel inferior will resort to "running the other down" in order to elevate himself or herself. The more the competition, the more the jealousy or envy between two persons, the more will the one seek to push the other down. You have had the experience, no doubt, of suddenly realizing in the course of a conversation that you have been subconsciously asking yourself, "What can I find wrong with this person?" You were probably angry with yourself on realizing how "gossipy" you had become. But the pertinent question is, "Why should I have to disparage the other?" Which means, what inferiority feeling is there in myself that should make me strive to pull the other down in order to raise myself?

Mental transference not only consists of negative, hostile ideas, but can as well carry a positive, friendly content. When talking with a loved individual, one senses affirmative, complimentary attitudes in the mind of the other. This is basic in the building up of love. *People could not fall in love without making use of the process of empathy.* All through history, lovers have been convinced that much more communication was occurring between them than merely the spoken word or the physical expression.

Trust and confidence and other aspects of good rapport increase the effectiveness of empathy. Empathy works best of all between persons in love; here is a condition of identification of psychic states that goes on day after day, until it becomes literally impossible to draw a demarcation where the personality of one leaves off and that of the other begins. Hostility, competition, and antagonism decrease the possibilities of empathy. Continued negative attitudes make empathy, even simple understanding, impossible between the persons concerned. One cannot understand one's enemy so long as the enemy is one's enemy. Thus, though empathy is a means of the transfer of both hostile and friendly attitudes between people, the former breaks down the connections and progressively destroys the possibilities of empathy, while the latter increasingly strengthens the attachment. *The secret of successful personal relations is the use of empathy in this constructive, affirmative, friendly, and upbuilding form.*

In conclusion, we state that the counselor and counselee may fruitfully assume that such mental transference takes place, and that there is therefore no room for anything but honesty. This means frankly that each will sense what the other is thinking, so there is no point in wasting time trying to deceive each other. They can assume that their minds and hearts are as open to view though they were placed on the table between them. This assumption means a breaking down of barriers. The counselor then refrains from playing any little game of deceit with the counselee, and the latter realizes that he or she will accomplish nothing by similar devices. This is the real meaning of honesty—a demolishing of barriers until someone takes another for what one really is. It amounts, of course, to a "nakedness" in the presence of the other; but there is no more cleansing experience in the world than psychological nakedness.

And finally, this is the real meaning of sincerity—a being "without wax," which is the derivation of the word. It is an attitude very close, if one may say so, to what Jesus had in mind when he spoke of the single-minded, the pure in heart, and those whose answer was a simple yea or nay.

3
The Secret of Influence

The discussion of empathy brings us finally to the subject of influence. This word is glibly bandied about by educators and ministers and others who realize that their aim is in the end to influence people, but rarely has the meaning of the term been given careful analysis. The popular writings on "how to influence" usually exhibit a very superficial understanding of what the process actually consists of, and thus much of the advice may be downright dangerous. Influence is a process which works chiefly in the unconscious. Better understanding of it would enable us better to protect ourselves and others from the insidious and vicious effects of the various waves of propaganda which attack our civilization like diseases.

Influence is one of the results of empathy. Wherever there is empathy some influence will be occurring, and wherever there is influence we can expect to find some identification of psychic states. The word has its root in the primitive astrological idea that an "in-flowing" of ethereal fluid from the stars affected the actions of people, which is the early mythological recognition of the fact that influence occurs in deep levels of the unconscious. Dictionary definitions include such synonyms as "induction," "effusion," "emanation," all of which are various empathetic processes.

Let us endeavor here to analyze influence as it appears in its different forms. There is first the *influence of ideas*. At the beginning of a year, to cite an example, I addressed a young people's group to which I was acting as adviser, on a certain subject. This same subject came up again for discussion somewhat by accident six months later. The young people presented ideas almost identical with those I had suggested months earlier; they had forgotten in the meantime the origin of the ideas and defended them vehemently as their very own brain children. Everyone working with people will have observed similar influence of ideas, in which other persons absorb the ideas and make them their own.

A second form of influence is that which we might term the *temporary influence of personality*. One often notices the curious fact that two persons talking together tend to take on the gestures, tones of voice, and general psychic states of each other. If the one has burst into the room heatedly and speaks in an excited voice, the other tends to take on this nervous tension. But if the second refuses to become excited and talks in a calm, leisurely manner, the first person gradually loses the nervous tension and absorbs some of this poise. The same form of influence is evidenced in the way embarrassment spreads in a social group, one embarrassed person passing on the contagion to the others until all become tense. This is all quite understandable; according to the principle of empathy it is impossible that two or more persons engage in genuine conversation without approximating each other's psychic states.

A hint for counselors arises from these observations: the skilled and sensitive counselor can put a counselee into a given mood, within certain limits, by assuming that mood. This is also the secret of many a successful hostess' or hosts' ability to put guests at ease.

There is also a *general influence of personality*, the more permanent form of what we have described above. This occurs when one individual assumes to some extent the personality pattern or role of another. The student, for example, will take on the tone of voice or peculiar manner of gesturing of a favorite professor. Members of a church often assume the mannerisms of their minister; and whole groups will exhibit behavior patterns, often very petty and inconsequential, which they have taken on from their leader. When one meets a disciple of a certain leader, one often has an uncanny, eerie feeling on observing that some small gestures of the disciple's are actually not the person's own but the leader's; and one feels that it is the leader and not the disciple standing before one just as *it is Hamlet and not the actor one sees on the stage*. The significant point is that this influence is ordinarily unconscious, the student or the disciple not realizing that he or she has taken on the gesture or tone or voice of the master.

How are we to explain influence?[9] Not as the result of mere contact, like water becoming blue when ink is poured into it. To be sure, the influencing is accomplished by certain items in the individual's environment; but the person *selects* these items, and by a very creative and mostly unconscious process. Since there are an infinite number of elements in every environment, an infinite number of persons can each receive a different influence from the same general environment.

Each individual, struggling as he or she is to attain a position of higher prestige and power, clutches at every rope in the form of a behavior pattern which gives promise of being of assistance in his or her upward movement. One sees other individuals succeeding in their movement toward the goal one has picked for oneself, and adopts their behavior patterns by unconscious or partially conscious imitation. It is along the line of the ego's striving for power that the individual is most open to influence. It is the vain person, for example, who is attracted by the lipstick and "become-beautiful-quickly" advertisements; and the sickly child may take as a hero the police officer or the famous general who possesses the great power he or she desires but does not have. When one person takes another as an "ideal" we may assume that the person wishes to attain the goal achieved by the other. This is a definitely emphatic process, the individual partially identifying with the ideal personality and thus playing the role and assuming the behavior patterns of the ideal person.

In religious and ethical education, it is well to remember that a boy or girl will not take the ideal held up as abstractly "good" or "recommended," but rather the one which gives the most promise of aiding him or her toward the position in life he or she wishes to attain. Under pressure youths may superficially and consciously accept the ideal held up by educators, but the ideal that deeply influences is that which is selected by processes in the unconscious. And the assuming of a different conscious ideal may militate against the unity of personality development and make for hypocrisy.[10] Empathetic identification on the part of the young person with some more ideal character is an entirely legitimate and efficacious method of ethical education, but it will come as an unconscious by-product of the identity of goals.

Since influence is a function of the individual's struggle for prestige and power, it follows that the person who has the power in a given relationship will exert the influence. In personal terms this power means *social courage*, which follows from such qualities as stability, maturity, and other aspects of clarification. It is the person in a given situation with the greater social courage who exerts the influence, and the person of lesser social courage who accepts it. Ordinarily, of course, the counselor holds the prestige by virtue of position as well as personality, and therefore exerts the major part of the influence in the counseling situation; but if the counselor is fatigued or for some other reason his or her courage is depressed, the tables may be turned. The counselor may assume the mood of the counselee and permit the other to direct the interview. In such case, the counselee is counseling the counselor! And the latter had best leave off the attempt to counsel until his or her courage has been restored.

The *truth factor* enters, of course, into any explanation of influence, particularly in respect to the influence of ideas. If the young people in the first example above had not believed the ideas true, they would not have accepted them. Uncritical observers, however, are inclined to overweight the truth factor, assuming that it is the only important explanation of influence; tell people the truth, they say, and that is all that is necessary. Unfortunately, our world is not so ideal. Groups are able to make themselves believe almost any piece of nonsense if it is in line with their ego striving. Truth is still on the scaffold—witness its mutilation in fascist countries. The public wants to be fooled, observes Adler, whom nobody could accuse of being a cynic; and we might add that individuals allow themselves to be persuaded of an obvious untruth because it raises their prestige to believe it. It is true that the individual must believe in the truth of the idea that is influencing him or her, but is able to go through a good many gymnastics of rationalization to accomplish this. *Convincingness* depends only partially, it is safe to conclude, upon the objective truth of the proposition at hand.

When we analyze a case of some pronounced influence, our question is not why the person had the power to influence the other, but rather what tendencies were there in the mind of the other, probably in the unconscious, which made the person so ready to be influenced? There must exist some unconscious readiness to believe, some predisposition toward the influence. Those who seek to protect youth from evil influences will best accomplish it not by sheltering them—this never works in our interdependent world—but rather by enabling them to achieve normal satisfactions and security in living so that they will not need to give in to the influences working on their wrong tendencies.[11]

We conclude by emphasizing several of the especially important implications for counselors. First, it is to be noticed that the *process of influence is unconscious on both sides*. The student is usually not aware of imitating a favorite professor's gestures and behavior patterns, and certainly the professor is not aware of it. The imitative process proceeds as part of the *"participation mystique."* It is as though the unconscious minds of the one doing the influencing and the one influenced were carrying on a conversation of which their conscious minds did not know. This brings home the eternal truism that it is what the counselor really is which exerts the influence, not the relatively superficial matter of the words being uttered. "What you are speaks so loudly that I cannot hear what you say."

The second implication is clear; as counselors or teachers or ministers, *we bear a responsibility*. We shall be influencing others whether they or we wish it or not, and we had best frankly recognize this. The teacher or minister is like a magnetic force on the campus or community; lines of force go out from him or her much farther than we ever imagine. If a counselor is especially neurotic in tendency, he or she will be like the bearer of a contagious disease; and everyone in the school or community will be exposed to the infectious neurosis. But one who has become courageous and socially minded will be like a purifying sun; and the whole community will be disinfected and made healthier by the cleansing rays. "All these guiding principles in therapy," Jung says in regard to the therapist, "confront the doctor with important ethical duties which can be summed up in the single rule: be the man through whom you wish to influence others."[12]

A final implication presses home: *as counselors we need to develop our capacity to empathize*. This involves learning to relax, mentally and spiritually as well as physically, learning to let one's self go into the other person with a willingness to be changed in the process. It is a dying to one's self in order to live with others. It is the great giving up of one's self, losing one's own personality temporarily and then finding it a hundredfold richer in the other person. "Except a grain of wheat fall into the earth and die. . . ."

*"The longer I live the more do human beings appear to be
fascinating and full of interest. . . .*

*"Foolish and clever, mean and almost saintly, diversely unhappy—
they are all dear to my heart; it seems to me that I do not properly
understand them and my soul is filled with an inextinguishable interest
in them. Many of them whom I knew are dead; I am afraid that except
me there is no one who will tell their story as I would like to do and
dare not; it will seem as though such men had never existed on earth at all. . . .*

*"The people I am most fond of are those who are not quite
achieved; who are not very wise, a little mad, 'possessed.' 'The people of
a sound mind' have little interest for me. The achieved man, the one
perfect like an umbrella, does not appeal to me. I am called and doomed,
you see, to describe—and what could I say of an umbrella but that is is
of no worth on a sunny day?*

*"A man, slightly possessed, is not only more agreeable to me;
he is altogether more plausible, more in harmony with the general tune
of life, a phenomenon unfathomed yet, and fantastic, which makes it
at the same time so confoundedly interesting."*

MAXIM GORKI   "Two Stories"
The Dial, September, 1927, pp. 197–98

PART

TWO

*Practical
Steps*

V   *Reading Character*

THE COUNSELOR'S DISTINGUISHING mark is a special sensitivity to people—sensitivity to their hopes and fears and personality tensions. Particularly, the counselor is sensitive to all the little expressions of character, such as tone of voice, posture, facial expression, even dress and the apparently accidental movements of the body. And so he or she learns to read character—not nearly so simply as the proverbial open book, but like a traveler going through a new country, finding everything new and interesting and trying to understand.

Everything about the person adds its stroke to the painting of the personality picture. Nothing, not even the smallest movement or change in expression, is meaningless or accidental; the inner personality is continually expressing itself in voice and gesture and dress, and the only question is the counselor's ability to perceive these expressions and sense something of their meaning. The personality pattern shows itself in an individual's every activity. It may be very obvious in external expressions, as, for instance, the way the person looks at another person, the manner of shaking hands, or of speaking. The whole personality may give an indelible impression, one way or another, which we sense almost intuitively.[1]

In this chapter we shall list a number of guiding points for the reading of character.[2] But first a caution must be stated: these expressions of character mean something slightly different with every individual, and hence the counselor should be *very tentative in drawing conclusions*. The matter is somewhat paradoxical; for though every gesture or facial expression is significant, it is the symptom—like the buoy on the water's surface—which leads in every case to a unique personality pattern, and hence the gestures and expressions of any two persons are never to be interpreted in exactly the same way.

We may here state a general caution for counselors: *hypotheses about an individual's personality pattern are to be made only from a constellation of many different factors*. Posture and tone of voice, position in the family, the particular problem the individual describes, relations to friends and to the opposite sex, success or failure in work—all of these and many more are pointer readings which indicate something, but no one in itself is sufficient basis for a conclusion. No two or three or four, in fact, are sufficient. Only when one has a number of pointer readings indicating much the same thing can one begin to set up hypotheses.

The *approach* of the counselee gives the counselor a first glimpse into his or her character. A firm, steady step indicates courage; whereas a hesitant step, telling that the individual has to renew resolution at every moment, indicates timidity and a general desire to withdraw from this interview. My counseling office in a college position happened to be at the end of a hall, and merely hearing the student walk down this hall and knock on my door gave me an impression of what he or she was going to be like. One student, for example, would come a few steps down the hall, pause a moment, and then proceed a few steps further; on arriving at the door, the student would knock in that apologetic way of one who hopes no one is in. Another type of student would stride down the hall, putting each foot down with a definite noise like a hero making an opening entrance on the stage, knock at the door briskly, and probably open it to enter without waiting for an invitation.

The manner of *shaking hands* has long been recognized as a significant expression of attitude and character. The "fishy" handshake, withdrawn immediately, is almost equivalent to the individual's saying, "I don't want to meet you." Such a person may act timidly toward all people, or may simply be afraid of this particular interview. The rough, strong handshake, in which the other person grips one's hand like a vise and pumps it enthusiastically as though to impress one that he or she is a direct descendant of sturdy pioneer stock, may be merely an effort to compensate for some deep inferiority feeling. The handshake is a symbol of union between persons; and it is a sign of personality health when it expresses genuine friendliness, interest in the other person, and a readiness to give.

The significance of *dress* is proverbial; and human beings have schooled themselves for many a century in reading the meaning of dress. It is not true that "clothes make the man," but it is true that details of attire give important hints about the attitudes of the person wearing the clothing. Freud explains this from the psychotherapeutic point of view: "Of equal significance to the physician and worthy of his observation, is everything that one does with his clothing, often without noticing it. Every change in the customary attire, every little negligence, such as an unfastened button, every trace of exposure means to express something that the wearer of the apparel does not wish to say directly; usually he is entirely unconscious of it."[3]

Slovenliness of dress, the need of a haircut, broken shoelaces and so on, tell us things the meaning of which no one can mistake. On the other hand, the person who is too meticulous about attire, whose fingernails are always filed perfectly and whose tie is always straight, is apt at the same time to have a too great care for details in other realms of living. Many individuals who develop what we term in a later chapter the religious or compulsion neurosis, exhibit in their dress this exaggerated desire that everything be perfectly neat and tidy and above reproach.

The woman who paints her fingernails green, or the one who uses too much makeup, is telling us by this means that she wants our attention. Either she does not receive enough genuine social attention or she has been pampered into demanding too much; and in either case the painting should be approached as a symptom of deeper maladjustments in the woman's personality.

Counselees who are particularly anxious about the interview often pay special attention to their attire before coming. When a woman counselee, for example, arrives obviously primped for the occasion, the counselor can infer that she has been anticipating this interview and is concerned about it. Of course, her primping may indicate a subjective, probably unconscious, interest in a male counselor, and it then becomes even more important that he read the meaning of her careful grooming in order to guard against the subjective element in the interview. The individual who comes carelessly dressed to a party is telling us by the same token that he or she does not care much about the group at the party. And a habitual lack of care for one's appearance indicates a general lack of interest in other people.

Reading the meaning of *distances* is another help toward understanding individuals. If the counselee takes a chair near the counselor, we can infer a friendly attitude; whereas sitting farther away indicates the existence of a barrier. This is Adler's interpretation of the meaning of distances, which I should call a sort of "geometry of love." Friendliness and interest and other aspects of love are indicated by a movement *toward*, whereas hate and the negative emotions are shown in movements *away from*. In our society, of course, persons have themselves so well under control that these movements are not at all obvious; but the counselor can observe even a slight flip of the head, or an almost imperceptible shying of one person from or toward another. The norm and ideal of personality health are in this case a free movement *toward*, the open-armed attitude toward life, or, in other words, an attitude of objective love. The neurotic individual, who is always exhibiting the movement *away from*, is precisely the one who cannot love.

One way of "reading" another's thoughts is simply to observe these very slight muscular reactions to ideas that course through the person's mind. Every thought, theoretically, has its counterpart in some muscular change in the body; and if one can read these expressions—which are very simple in the matter of smiling and frowning—one has developed a capacity very useful in the understanding of other people's characters.

There are many signs by which one can observe nervousness during the interview, such as the counselee's crossing and recrossing of legs, or grasping the arms of the chair tightly, or holding himself or herself taut in any way. In such cases, we ask ourselves, why does this individual have to be nervous; what, in other words, is the person hiding or inwardly struggling with? And the answer to these questions will lead us into his personality problem.

Facial expressions are, of course, of great importance in the reading of character. Most human beings have developed the ability to read with some accuracy the meaning of the spontaneous facial expressions of their associates, but they ordinarily find it impossible to see through a feigned expression. The counselor should be able to read joy and pain and fear as expressed in a person's face; but on the other hand, he or she should also be able to detect pain even though the other simulates poise and ease. The person who is always smiling is probably exhibiting a false optimism. The one who is invariably perfectly posed outwardly is probably compensating for an actual fear of the situation.

I have been interested in observing the characteristics of the faces of neurotics, in photographs and in person; and I shall offer here some of my observations, which may be suggestive though they are not at all to be considered final rules. The ends of the mouth of a neurotic individual often turn down. This makes the "long" face which is the expression of pessimism, despondency, and lack of social interest. We should expect such an individual to be slow in his or her movements, to make negative, sarcastic comments, and to exhibit a general lack of decisiveness. The eyes of neurotics are often taut and held more widely open than normal, which is the general expression of the frightened individual. The color of many neurotics is pallid and sickly; this is quite understandable, for the neurotic attitude means a general lowering of vitality, and the person tends to become actually sick physically because of mental turmoil. The neurotic expression seems to be very similar to the expression all of us wear in moments of great fatigue, or even fright or worry.

Dostoevski, keen student of human nature that he was, has aptly observed: "One can recognize a person's character much better by his laughter than by a boring psychological examination."[4] It is significant that the neurotic individual finds it very difficult to laugh. He or she can sneer or be sardonic and ironic and leer like the villains in the old-style dramas—for in these expressions, the corners of the mouth still turn *down*—but cannot genuinely laugh. True laughter is the expression of mental health. It is an invitation to friendliness, a true proof of the open-armed attitude toward life.

The *tone of voice* can tell us much, for there is music in a voice which expresses as definite a mental and spiritual attitude as a piece of symphonic music. Often one can tell merely by the tone of voice what a speaker means even if no known words are used. Sincerity is shown in a clear voice, courage in a steady one, and an interest in people in the voice that is so distinct that no one can escape contact with it. Certainly the individual who mouths words or talks so quietly that you must strain to hear does not want to make contact with you.

Nervousness and emotional turmoil are shown most clearly in the voice. If the counselee speaks slowly and with great control, like George B. in the case in the first chapter, we can infer that special psychological tensions exist in his mind. We have already noted how repressions and inhibitions can be tracked down by observing at what words the individual hesitates or gets confused or repetitious. Or if the counselee "protests too much," we may doubt whether the person actually believes what he or she is saying. By this overstressing of the point, he or she gives proof of the existence in his or her own unconsciousness of doubts as to the truth of the statement (proof of trying to persuade himself or herself as well as the listener). With his customary astuteness, Freud points out that when a writer or speaker uses an involved and round-about style, we may rightly ask what that person is trying to put over on us. Honesty in speech means directness, and one who labors the point or exhibits a nervous voice or employs indirection may be trying to attack us from the rear.

1
Forgetting and Slips

It is not our purpose to delve deeply into those most fascinating and rewarding subjects, memory and forgetting, and slips of speech and faulty actions, as the counselor does not deal directly with these expressions of the counselee's unconsciousness. But a counselor should, however, possess some general intelligence concerning the meaning of such phenomena if he or she is to understand human nature at all profoundly.

One does not forget by accident. The hostess who remarks to the guest, "Oh, I'm so sorry; I forgot you were coming," or the person who pleads, "Do forgive me; I'm no good at remembering names," is begging forgiveness actually under false pretenses; and the guest and the person whose name is forgotten are right in being offended. Memory works with a purpose. Within the unconsciousness of the individual, a selective process goes on which sorts out those things desired to be remembered prominently and puts away other things. Nothing, it is probably safe to say, is ever really forgotten. Our problem, then, is why certain things are tossed to the forefront of the mind, while others are pushed so far back that the individual can recall them only with effort, or perhaps not at all.

In his earliest work, Freud noticed this curious purposiveness in forgetting. He interpreted it in terms of the pleasure-pain sifting, concluding that the individual forgets those things which are associated with something unpleasant. Thus the mechanism of forgetting gave Freud an entrance to the understanding of the unconscious. But Freud's explanation is incomplete; often we remember most vividly precisely those experiences which caused us most pain, such as a humiliating and embarrassing social *faux pas*. Adler went deeper by pointing out that the individual remembers those experiences which have a special significance for his or her style of life.[5] Out of this insight Adler developed one of his most useful contributions to psychotherapeutic analysis—his famous use of the *early childhood memory* as an avenue to the understanding of the style of life[6] of the person. We may explain this as follows: a thousand things happened to John Doe, let us say in his third or fourth year of infancy, but he forgot all the other experiences and remembered this one. Why should this one image be selected in his unconsciousness and hung up like a guidepost in the forefront of his memory all these years? Clearly, this early childhood memory must possess some peculiar significance, and it possesses this significance regardless of whether it is a true happening or an imagined one. Adler concluded that such an early memory is a little closeup snapshot, if rightly interpreted, of the individual's personality pattern.

This theory turns out to be true practically as well as theoretically, for very often we can see in the early memory the same general tendencies which the personality pattern of the individual manifests twenty years later. The understanding of the early memories can be of value to counselors, as will be pointed out in the next chapter, given sufficient tentativeness and caution in interpretation.

Slips of speech and faulty actions, like memory and forgetting, are expressions of the unconsciousness of the individual. In these phenomena the unconscious material springs into expression in spite of the conscious censorship; it gets by the watchdog in a sudden leap. It has become common banter to interpret one's companion's slips of speech, and to amuse a parlor group by "psycho-scandalizing" people on the basis of these slips. The interpretations given in this bantering are apt to be wrong, but the underlying theory—namely, that a slip in speech actually says what one really is thinking but did not intend to say—is quite accurate. We have all had experiences similar to that of a friend of mine who was introducing a line of sorority members to a very notable person when one approached bedecked in an impossibly large hat; my friend, much to her horror and the amusement of the group, introduced her as "Miss Hat."

One could recount such stories endlessly; but we shall merely point out the basic consideration, that all slips of speech and faulty actions are to be viewed as having a meaning even though that meaning may be too recondite for the uninitiated to discover. The boy loses his schoolbooks, but not his fishing equipment. The student forgets his appointment with the professor, but his date with the new blonde sophomore, never! The housewife who is constantly misplacing or losing her keys, it has been aptly observed, has never become reconciled to the position of being a housewife.[7]

The interpretation of some phenomena in this field is not particularly difficult, and in such cases the counselor can justifiably use his or her observations. For example, if an individual is continually tardy for appointments or forgets them entirely, we are justified in hypothesizing that in his unconsciousness there exists an attitude of hesitancy, a tendency to withdraw from the subject in question. Or if a person continually forgets names, we may rightly infer that he lacks adequate social interest. The common remark, "I've never been any good at remembering names," might be translated into the more truthful, "I'm not particularly interested in people." In all of these generalizations there will appear many exceptions; but the generalization possesses some validity nevertheless, and will be useful to the skillful and cautious counselor.

The reader who wishes to delve more deeply into this most fascinating area of memory and slips and faulty actions will find an abundance of material.[8] Here let us merely point out that though the counselor does not use these phenomena like the psychotherapist as means of prying into the unconsciousness of the individual, he or she may with great profit aim to be intelligent about their meaning and thus increase his or her general understanding of human nature. Sometimes he or she will be able to interpret this meaning, more often not. In this realm the counselor is interested in *observing intelligently* rather than in drawing conclusions.

2
The Family Constellation

We have another valuable guide to the understanding of an individual's personality pattern, namely, his or her position in the family. It is quite understandable that this family position should be very significant; each person spends the first years, the most formative ones, almost entirely at the mercy of the family. The main lines of personality pattern are laid down very early in life, some psychologists say as early as the third year of infancy; and later character depends on the way a person uses this original pattern. In our endeavor to understand any person, it is therefore essential that we look to his or her position in the family constellation.

Fortunately we are able to discover some general tendencies connected with certain positions in the family constellation.[9] The *oldest child* in a family tends to have a prominent sense of responsibility. This child has enjoyed the entire love and solicitude of both parents during the first years, and this has lent the child a certain stability. He or she also has been entrusted with responsibility from earliest days, probably having been called upon to help the mother in little tasks and even in the bringing up of the other children. The oldest has likely been the recipient of the parents' confidences and a sharer in their planning to a much greater degree than the other children. The oldest child thus tends to uphold law and order, to be conservative and a lover of stability. We may think of him or her allegorically as trying to get back to that original state of the first years of infancy, sitting alone on the throne of the parents' affections.

This favored position of the eldest has long been recognized in folk customs in the tradition of passing the crown or the aristocratic title or even the peasant's plot of land down to the eldest son. Mrs. D., the oldest of five children, illustrates the characteristics of this position in the family. One of her earliest memories was assisting her mother in the household duties by picking up the paper. She used to help regularly in the care of the younger children, and her mother shared her plans with her even from a very early age. Now Mrs. D. occupies a position entailing considerable responsibility, and discharges her duties very creditably.

We find quite different tendencies in the *second child*, who comes into the world confronted by a rival who is already one or two years old. Through infancy and childhood he or she has always had to follow this pace setter who is able to walk and talk and do many things before he or she can. The second child thus has his or her inferiority reiterated vividly and continuously, and so acts like a racer trying to overtake the pace setter. But as fate has decreed it, the other child always has the advantage in growth and size, and the probability is that no matter how hard the second strives, he or she will not be able to catch up. This child may seize upon a special realm of activity in which to better the elder. The situation is complicated, also, by the fact that the elder may become jealous, regarding the second as an upstart who came to dethrone the elder in their parent's affections. All of these attitudes are deeply buried in the unconsciousness, of course; and oftentimes the individual will never admit this rivalry with a brother or sister even though objective signs indicate it clearly.

The second child, then, tends to develop an exaggerated ambition and the habit of striving at a great tension. He or she tends also to be the revolutionary; his or her early situation was not of the best, and we can picture the second child, again allegorically, as desirous of upsetting the applecart and starting things off again on a more even footing. The counselor often encounters vivid examples of this inferiority-ambition pattern of the second child. George B., the tremendously ambitious reformer of the case study in Chapter 1, was, we remember, the second child following a girl, which makes the situation more serious because girls develop physically more quickly than boys in the early years.

Those between the second and the youngest child occupy positions which are less significant, and there is little that can be predicted about them. But the *youngest child* has been recognized all through history as standing in a special position. In many fairy tales it is the youngest daughter who marries the prince, or the youngest son who by unusual ability achieves greatness and becomes the savior of the family.

This youngest child has ordinarily been the recipient of an unusual amount of affection during infancy and youth, not only from the parents but from older brothers and sisters as well. All these grown-ups have helped the youngest, done things for, taken care of and no doubt endeavored to instruct and educate him or her. This may give the youngest child a particularly affectionate attitude toward the world and a general expectancy that he or she will love and be loved by everybody. We all know youngest children who are extraordinarily likable. But the danger is that they become especially pampered, and consequently expect the world always to coddle and comfort them. And when they find it does not, they may take on a neglected and pouting attitude. Miss R., an example of the youngest child, was a person of unusual charm and attractiveness. But her personality difficulty lay in her expectation that the world be too beautiful, good, and ideal; and she tended to become cynical and distrustful when her hopes were disappointed.

The youngest child may, on the other hand, interpret the situation as one of inferiority, since his or her world is made up of powerful adults; and may consequently develop a strong ambition and vow that upon growing up he or she will surpass all the others.

And now concerning the *only child*. People have recognized for ages how difficult this position is. The entire love and solicitude of the parents have been heaped upon this child; they have been particularly watchful lest anything happen to their only baby; and the child thus receives much more attention and educative effort than children who have brothers and sisters. This only child, too, does not have the experience of social contacts, of learning to live with other individuals, which children of larger families receive. All of this means that this child has the most likelihood of being pampered and thereby developing a demanding and dependent attitude toward life. This person may expect the world to come to him or her, as indeed his or her infant's world did. And when it does not, he or she may secretly feel betrayed, and take on a resentful and uncourageous attitude toward life.

The picture facing the only child is not, however, entirely bleak. Only children have greater possibilities for development than other children; for they have been the recipients of the combined educative efforts of both parents, and they will have had more opportunities for self-development. Greater dangers, in the case of the only child as in all personality development, go hand in hand with greater possibilities.

Helen M. was an only child. Until she was twenty-seven, her parents had made most of her decisions. Her father had showered her with affection, but had been dominating at the same time; and her earliest memory was of his spanking her all the way home after she had got lost. We note here a mistake that parents often make—that of bestowing unusual affection on the child and yet disciplining severely at the same time, both of which tend to spoil the child. Such parents are especially strict and severe with the child because they see the danger in their loving too much, then return with great affection to balance their disciplining, and so on until the poor child does not know what to make of this strange world. When Helen M. went away to college she was troubled by an oppressive inferiority feeling although she was actually very attractive. We observe here that the inferiority feeling is not an index of one's actual inferiority, but a special interpretation the individual makes of his or her situation; in many cases, it is merely a technique by which one separates one's self from one's social group. Miss M. had difficulty making contacts with other students on the campus, and consequently kept up her practice of running home frequently. After graduation, she obtained a teaching job; but such was the strain of this situation where she had to be independent and make decisions for herself that, even though she lived at home, she suffered long weeping spells, often could not go to sleep at night, and was on the verge of a nervous breakdown. At the time of this counseling she was twenty-eight, unmarried, and not even in love. The superficial observer, noticing her attractiveness, would be surprised at this. But the more profound student of human nature knows that courage and the ability to make important decisions are prerequisite even to falling genuinely in love, let alone getting married; and the pampered child lacks these qualities. Miss M. reported that she had been "sublimating" her sexual instinct—which, as we shall discuss in a later chapter, is a common means of escaping responsibility for solving one's sexual problem. She was a very intelligent woman, however; and through her understanding of herself and her situation, we can expect that she will be able to develop the necessary courage and independence, and thus put her talents and capabilities to socially constructive work and at the same time solve the problem of her love life creatively.

Other positions in the family constellation, we shall remark in conclusion, have particular effects upon the individual. Twins, for example, often tend to develop in opposition to each other, each choosing different lines in which to specialize and surpass. A boy growing up in a family of girls will exhibit certain tendencies, as will a girl born into a family of boys. Sometimes the counselor can obtain valuable hints by discovering which members of the family the counselee was most attached to and those with whom he or she did not get along.

By understanding the family background we are able to see the counselee's character in perspective. We seek the road down which each has traveled, and thus we are much better able to understand his or her condition upon reaching us. The direction in which the counselee is moving then becomes clearer to us; and this movement is the concern, in our dynamic understanding of personality, which is of most interest. Sometimes when counseling I get sudden glimpses of this person at six or ten or twenty, almost as vividly as if he or she were to be transformed into childhood form for a moment before me. As counselor I never permit myself to set up any hypotheses about an individual until I know the background; in fact, one could not, as it is like trying to solve an equation with one number missing. In cases where this background cannot be ascertained—as when one conjectures about the weary person sitting opposite on a bus—one finds oneself automatically hypothesizing an imaginary background.

It should remain clear that the family background is not to be thought of as a total *cause* of the individual's present situation. We must not slip into an easy determinism at this point. A counselee may try to blame a present difficulty on something in the childhood environment, but to the extent that the counselee thinks of himself or herself still as a product of cause and effect his or her readjustment of personality will be thwarted. It is the counselor's function—after admitting all the force of the childhood environment, and in fact pointing out to the counselee many aspects of this influence which the counselee has not suspected—to indicate insistently that the present concern is how this background is to be *used* for the most creative adjustment. Granted that the eldest tends to be conservative, there is no limit to the socially constructive use to which this tendency, in the form of social responsibility, can be put. And granted that the second tends to be revolutionary; many of society's greatest benefactors, and individuals who achieved a very creative adjustment of their personality tensions, have been reformers who turned their ambitions to the service of humanity. The individual's background is an aid to understanding, but not a total explanation. The locus of the personality problem still remains within the inmost area of the individual's free creativity.

As you have been reading this chapter, you have no doubt been feeling that many of the observations were far-fetched, and possibly even a little dangerous. So we shall conclude, as we began, with the caution that hypotheses about an individual's personality pattern are to be drawn only from a constellation of many different factors. All the considerations we have been describing—the counselee's posture, manner of speaking, family position, early childhood memory, what he or she now forgets or slips in speech, the nature of the present problem—all of these tell something to the alert counselor. When a majority of these pointer readings indicate the same thing, the counselor can begin to set up a hypothesis, but not before. We use the term "hypothesis" advisedly, because one never draws final conclusions when dealing with a personality; the material is not that static. I have found it advisable to juggle the observations about in my mind, putting off the forming of a hypothesis until suddenly the facts fall into line as though by themselves.

The purpose of this chapter has been to sensitize the counselor. We do not wish to outfit the counselor with a set of rules—heaven forbid! We wish rather to help him or her to become alert to the infinite number of ways of "feeling out" character, and to render the counselor so sensitive to people that this reading— shall we say *appreciating*—of their characters becomes second nature. To every generalization offered above there are all kinds of exceptions; our discussion has aimed to suggest and stimulate rather than to codify. And there are thousands of ways of understanding character which we have not even touched upon. It is our hope that counselors will endeavor to explore these ways by themselves. To understand people—that is the counselor's job.

Is there danger in this emphasis upon reading other peoples' character? Will they object, as is sometimes argued, if you continually "study" them? Of course, if you go about it like one peeking into another's private room. This sort of "analysis" is directly opposite to what we have been talking about; it is actually done because the analyst wishes to set himself or herself above other people by "getting their number." The true counselor goes at it altogether differently. He or she seeks to understand people from the standpoint of appreciation. And far from objecting, people prize this kind of understanding. It raises the prestige of the one who is understood, and helps give a sense of worth as a person. This understanding breaks down the barriers which separate people; it draws the other human being for a moment out of the loneliness of individual existence and welcomes the person into community with another soul. It is like inviting the traveler in from a snowy and chilly journey to sit for an hour before the fire of another's hearth. Such understanding, it is not too much to say, is the most objective form of love. That is why there is always a tendency on the part of the counselee to feel some love toward the counselor, this person "who understands me."

There are few gifts that one person can give to another in this world as rich as understanding.

VI

Confession
and Interpretation

CONTACT HAVING BEEN made with the counselee, and rapport having been established, we now find ourselves in the central stage of the interview, the *confession*. This stage consists of the counselee's "talking it out." It is the *piece de resistance* of both counseling and psychotherapy. So important, in fact, is the confession that counselors can well hold themselves to the practice initiated by the psychotherapists; namely, that of reserving at least two-thirds of every hour for talking on the part of the counselee.

After the counselee has talked out his or her problem, described the situation, and laid all the cards on the table, the *interpretation* stage takes place. During this period, both counselee and counselor survey the facts that have been brought to light and endeavor to discover through them the personality pattern of the counselee, wherein lie the sources of maladjustment. Interpretation is a function of both counselor and counselee working together. In the confession stage, the counselee occupies the limelight and does practically all the talking. But in the interpretation the counselor becomes increasingly prominent, first merely by asking leading questions, then by offering suggestive insights, and, finally, by empathetic influence upon the counselee.

Probably the most fruitful approach will be to illustrate the confession and interpretation stages by narrating an actual interview. I shall therefore describe a two-hour interview, in very condensed form, using as much as possible the exact words of the counselee and counselor. This case is selected because the counselee in question was particularly intelligent, and therefore the interpretation could proceed without waste of time. But for that very reason the case is not to be regarded as typical, as most counselees will require a much slower process. At the end of the narration, we shall sum up and examine the more important points emerging in the interview.

1
Case of Bronson

Mr. Bronson, as we shall term our counselee, was a college instructor in philosophy of religion. When he came for counseling, I noticed that he was an attractive, intelligent-appearing young man. He shook my hand cordially and smiled in a friendly way. We exchanged a few sentences and then, without the customary procrastination, he went immediately into his problem.

Bronson: I am troubled by the fact that I always work at a great tension. I can't seem to relax. When I let up at all, I get sick. It's rather strange—the second day of every vacation I feel myself all done out, and have to go to bed with a cold or something of the sort. (*He laughs.*)

Counselor: Well, that's interesting. Tell me more about it.

Bronson: It seems as though I must always have something driving me, something compelling me to keep at my work. If I don't have this strong outside compulsion, I just slump altogether.

Counselor: You mean driving you in your teaching?

Bronson: Yes, but also in other aspects of my work, such as writing articles. When I have to write a book review, for example, I read the book, make a *precis* of it, fuss over it, throw myself into the writing; and then after spending a lot of time on it, I put it away and never finish it. As a matter of fact, I must have a dozen unfinished articles lying around my office, which I have never used.

Counselor: Yes, you do appear to work at a great strain. How long have you noticed this tension?

(*By this time the counselor has observed some of the external manifestations of the counselee's character. Bronson sits in a friendly manner, not appearing at all hostile. But his movements are jerky and definitely nervous, and from time to time he pulls one leg up and sits on it in a taut position. His eyes have a somewhat faded and fatigued appearance, and his complexion is pallid.*)

Bronson: Always. At least, ever since I can remember. In high school I worked very hard and fast—I was quite small then, only four feet ten; and I had to use my brains to get what I wanted. So I did good work scholastically. Then when I went to college, I continued to work at the same tension and have kept it up ever since. I've always had something of an economic problem, which didn't help matters.

Counselor: Tell me more about how this tension appears in your living now.

Bronson: The main trouble is that I cannot get accomplished what I want to. When I have to do something, such as correcting papers, I put it off and pick up something else which is more interesting. And finally, when the last moment comes, I throw myself into the work with great fury and get it done in a burst of speed. I work in this tense manner on articles, too; but with them I feel I must always do a little more, read another book or two, or rewrite the article because it isn't perfect; and consequently I never get it finished.

Counselor: But have you never thought that you could do better creative work if you did not keep yourself at this great tension?

Bronson: Yes, I have realized that often. But at other times I feel that I must have something compelling me from the outside. I have a great horror of ever getting into a position where I would not have these external drives, for then I would go to seed immediately. I feel I do better teaching when I throw myself into it with great energy.

(*We note here an inconsistency in the counselee's thought; he complains that working at the great strain causes his difficulties, yet he feels that the outside compulsions are useful, and he appears desirous of retaining them. This inconsistency shows us that the tensions of which he complains are really symptoms of some maladjustment deeper in his personality. His statement that he works better under strain is not to be taken at its face value, for he would be forced to rationalize the matter in some such way as this.*)

But it's pretty hard on me. The night before I gave my first lecture in philosophy I didn't sleep a wink. And it was the same the night before I substituted for Professor Brown in his lecture; and I was terribly nervous and upset in the class even though I knew all the students.

(*We observe from the material so far that Mr. Bronson is not particularly abnormal. He occupies a good position and is what the world calls a successful young man. But he is potentially neurotic and could slip into neurosis at any time the pressure was sufficient, as we shall see below. More important, we notice that his personality difficulty is distinctly inhibiting his creative accomplishment. In this respect he clearly needs to be "liberated."*)

The counselor's purpose in this case, then, is to help Mr. Bronson to readjust his personality tensions so that first, the possibility of his going neurotic in the future will be lowered, and second, his creative powers will be freed.)

Counselor: Have you ever had a breakdown under these strains?

Bronson: Yes, when I was a senior in college I had a nervous collapse. I had just got engaged, and that made me strive all the harder. Suddenly I went off into a sort of dreamy state—I couldn't study, couldn't do anything. They sent me with my sister down to the ocean, where we stayed for three months. I was in a comatic state; I went to sleep, woke up, but did practically nothing else. But finally I came back to college and finished out the year. Another time . . . (*Here Bronson begins to laugh.*) Once I had a terrible time. I was phoned one night to take a fairly important Bible class on the following morning. I didn't know much about the subject, but I couldn't get out of it. I stayed up all night, all my muscles taut and my body as nervous as could be, drinking coffee and trying to look over some notes. But I got nothing done. Next morning I got on the bus in a fuddle, scarcely knowing what I was doing. I felt a strange pain at the base of my brain, as though something were going wrong. While riding the bus I looked across at the Jersey shore and felt a strong desire—(*he emphasizes the point*) honestly, a pull that was almost too strong to be resisted, to take the train to New Jersey and escape the whole thing.

Counselor: (*laughing*) Well, you did get pretty close to the line.

Bronson: (*also laughing*) Yes, I know that's the way people go crazy—if I'd waked up in California and not known how I got there, they'd have locked me up in the asylum for sure. But I didn't go to New Jersey. When I got to the class I saw it consisted of a bunch of old ladies whom nobody should be afraid of, and so I walked in and got off some old drivel. But, boy, that was an experience!

(So far the interview consists entirely of confession, the counselee merely "talking it out." This goes on much longer than is here recorded. Now the counselor must elicit certain necessary information from the counselee.)

Counselor: What is your age, Bronson? And tell me something, if you will, about your family and your position in it.

Bronson: I am twenty-six. I am the second child in our family, my sister being two years older. My father is a minister.

(The counselee also gives the information that he married at twenty and has had entirely happy relations with his wife. Evidently the sex factor does not play a prominent role in this maladjustment.)

Counselor: You appear to have a tremendously strong ambition. *(This marks the beginning of the stage of* interpretation. *The counselor will now seek to point out various relationships in the personality in the endeavor to find the underlying pattern.)*

Bronson: Yes, I am very ambitious. I have always worked very hard to succeed.

Counselor: Now we know that an exaggerated ambition, when the individual is not able to let up his striving, is very often connected with some deep inferiority feeling . . .

Bronson: *(interrupting)* I certainly have had an inferiority complex. It was connected with my being so small in high school, and I had to strive hard to make a place for myself. And, also, I've always associated with people older than I was. In school I was always a couple of years ahead of the boys my age.

Counselor: Do you know what your position in the family indicates?

(Bronson does not; so the counselor explains briefly how the second child tends to develop a prominent ambition, and that this is accentuated when the older child is a girl.)

Bronson: Yes, this seems to fit my case perfectly. When I was very young I can remember always trying to outdo my sister. She was rather sickly; so that made it easier. I raised such a fuss when she went to school that my parents were forced to put me in school also, though I was only four at the time. One of the reasons I studied so hard was to get ahead of my sister.

(It is clear that Bronson is unusually objective about himself, and is able to grasp quickly the meaning of the relationships which the counselor points out. This, of course, expedites the counseling process.)

Counselor: Can you tell me an early childhood memory? (*He briefly explains the significance of such memories.*)
Bronson: Why, yes. I guess I was about two or three when this happened. I was pushed to the fair in a little cart in which I rode backwards. While we were at the fair the pole of the cart broke and the man who worked for us had to carry me all the way home. I also remember a dream I had many years ago. It clung so vividly to my mind that it seems like an early memory. I dreamt I was climbing up into the attic of our house on a ladder. When I got to the top rung, a monkey jumped out of a green box in the attic and scared me, and I fell down the ladder. (*He laughs. The counselor by this time sees the outlines of the personality pattern, and he explains his hypothesis to the counselee.*)
Counselor: That dream is very interesting. We can now see some rather distinct things about your personality pattern. Let me sum them up. You work at a great tension, you said, which keeps you under a nervous strain and interferes with your creative accomplishment. We agreed that this great tension was really the expression of an exaggerated ambition, and that this ambition was connected with your inferiority feeling. Your position in the family fits into this picture. And that dream gives us some hints, too—you remember, you climbed up the ladder to the top, and then fell. Have you always been afraid of falling, or let us say, of failing?
Bronson: Why, yes, as a matter of fact I have been—very much so.

(So far Bronson's personality pattern is the general inferiority-ambition-neurotic symptom form. Now the counselor must push the interpretation deeper to discover the unique aspects of this pattern and the consequent neurotic tendency.)

Counselor: Why should you be afraid of failure?

Bronson: I don't know. I never have failed in any outstanding matter. But I always fear I will.

Counselor: You appear to fear some catastrophe. This usually arises out of a basic distrust of life—a feeling that one must watch carefully or some disastrous thing will happen. Do you have that feeling?

Bronson: *(thinks a moment)* Yes, I've never thought of it in that way, but I guess I am distrustful and suspicious of life. I do have the feeling I must fight it all the time. You know, I've never been able to accept that statement "Be not anxious." I believe in God, but yet I have a fear and deep distrust—rather inconsistent, isn't it? *(Empathy has become very well established so that the counselor and counselee appear to be thinking along together.)*

Counselor: This distrust of life is connected with your inferiority feeling—they both represent a general feeling of insecurity. No wonder you feel you must be striving hard at all times. If you could relax that inferiority feeling, you would be able to use your creative powers more fruitfully.

Bronson: I think you're right. Now what steps shall I take to do this?

(This is a crucial point. The counselee asks for advice. If the counselor succumbs to the temptation, with its implicit flattery, and gives advice, or even specific instructions, he short-circuits the process and thwarts the real personality readjustment of the counselee, as will be explained in the next chapter. Rather, the counselor must seize this request for advice as a means of making the counselee accept more responsibility for himself.)

Counselor: You wish rules on the matter. You want these rules to compel you from the outside. And you'll follow them with the same strain and tension you manifest now. That will make your problem all the worse. Your desire for rules, you see, rises out of that same basic mistrust of life.

Bronson (*after a moment's pause*): Yes, I see that. But what am I to do?

Counselor: It is more a matter of relaxing the artificial tensions and giving your creative abilities a chance. And to do that you must understand yourself better and get over that basic distrust of life. Let's get back to the particular tension in your work which you originally described. You say you feel you must be driven from the outside?

Bronson: Well, as you said, it is connected with my family position. I got into the habit of striving too much when I was young, and I've just been keeping it up. (*Here he attempts to explain away the problem by means of his childhood environment, and to relieve himself of responsibility by blaming a bad habit for it.*)

Counselor: It does not help simply to blame the habit. The habit has something to do with your present difficulty, to be sure; but it's a deeper matter than merely the changing of a habit. It is more fruitful to assume that your present exaggerated tendency to strive arises out of the same factors in your personality pattern which gave rise to your similar striving ten years ago. (*A pause. The counselee has reached a temporary impasse; the matter goes deeper than he had expected. The counselor takes a different approach, but pointing toward the same center of the problem.*) You seem to have a strong desire for perfection coming out of your fear of failure. Do you have a dread of being imperfect?

Bronson: Yes, I do—very strongly so. That's why I never get my articles published—I think they're not perfect.

Counselor: But you realize that nobody achieves perfection in this world? Everybody fails at some time or other.

Bronson: Yes, that's right.

Counselor: You see, if you always demand perfection, you'll never do anything. You will never take the last step up that ladder for fear some monkey will drop out on you. One needs the courage of imperfection to live creatively. (*The conclusion of the*

*interview approaches. The counselor must sum up the diagnosis
and clinch it by taking advantage of the empathetic relationship
between him and the counselee.*)

Counselor: (*leaning forward and looking directly at the
counselee*): Why do you distrust life?

Bronson: I don't know. But the more I think about it, the
more I realize that I have always had this special feeling of insecurity and suspicion.

Counselor: We can understand this suspicion and distrust of
life as coming out of your inferiority feeling, which was accentuated by your small size in your youth and your family position. But you are no longer inferior—you occupy a good position and certainly enjoy more security than most people in the
world. So you do not need to fight life so desperately now. You
can afford to *trust* more. All these fears and staying awake nights
and the great strains are unnecessary. You can get along better
without them. That exaggerated fear of failure is a bogey; you
are not in danger of failing. The dream may have been true once,
but it is not now; and you don't need to be worried for fear a
monkey will jump out and scare you. So you can take on courage
and let this unnecessary inferiority feeling evaporate. You can
develop the courage of imperfection, and in that way you'll relax
much of that driving ambition. You need to give your creative
abilities a chance. That means trusting and affirming life more.
And it means affirming yourself, so that you will be able to create
without being forced from the outside.

(*Counselor and counselee have been looking directly at each
other. The latter reflects for a moment as he becomes aware of
the new possibilities before him. As he gets up to go, Bronson
expresses his gratitude to the counselor, and says, as he stands
at the door:*)

Bronson: Say, I think that distrust of life explains why I have
become so interested lately in supernatural theology. By this I
was able to look down on the world, and condemn man and conclude that the world was all bad and nothing could be expected
but catastrophe. I now see that this attitude is probably connected
with my general pessimism about life.

Counselor: Possibly it is; you know more about that than I. You might turn these questions over in your mind in the future— the questions of your basic distrust of life and why you feel you must be compelled from the outside. You'll continually get new insights into how your difficulties arise out of your personality pattern, and thus you'll become increasingly better able to understand yourself.

2
Aspects of Confession

Before we discuss the confession stage in general, let us make clear again that the above is not to be regarded as a typical case by which other interviews are to be judged. Bronson possessed much more ability to look at himself objectively than most counselees, and therefore the interview moved much more rapidly than we should ordinarily expect. Whereas this interview lasted two hours, it would customarily require three or perhaps four hour periods to penetrate as deeply into the personality pattern. Then, too, the factors in Bronson's personality fitted together unusually clearly. The counselor should be ready to expect ordinarily a more difficult task in discovering the basic relationships within the personality.

Let us note, also, that this case did not end with a cure. Its purpose was to illustrate confession and interpretation; and the matter of the cure—transformation—will be discussed in the next chapter. What we wished to do was to enlighten Bronson, to help him understand himself; and it was not at all expected that his personality would be remade when he stepped out the door. There was a process of transformation set in motion, of course, on the basis of *understanding* and *suggestion*, which are curative forces that we shall discuss below. But this interview did not vanquish

Bronson's difficulty—it fitted him, rather, to vanquish it for himself. What such an interview accomplishes is to be observed after a couple of months, when the suggestions have had time to work themselves out in the counselee's daily living.

Some important guides for the counselor arising from our general discussion of confession are, first, the principle that *the counselee does the talking* in the confession period. This point, of course, is obvious; but it must be stressed, for unless the counselee "talks it out" with some degree of thoroughness, the counseling will not get to the root of the matter. It can almost be made a rule: if the counselee does not do at least two-thirds of the talking in a given hour, something is wrong with the counseling procedure. The counselor should be chary about talking; every word the counselor utters should have a purpose.

It is well for us to realize, as the second guide, that there is a *cathartic value in confession per se*. The mere fact that the counselee has talked a problem out, in the presence of a presumably objective and understanding counselor, has made the counselee psychologically healthier. It has relieved him or her of some inhibitions; it has made possible a more ready flow from subconscious to consciousness by flushing the channel; and it has helped him or her see problems in the clarifying light of objectivity. This does not mean that confession to any person who happens to be at hand will bring the same reward, be it the cook in the fraternity house or a shepherd on the hillside. The function of empathy is such that the person to whom one is confessing has much to do with the cathartic value of the confession.

The skillful counselor is able to *turn the counselee's confession to the central problem*. Unlike Bronson, most counselees will tend to procrastinate and ramble about among minor topics, putting off the fated moment when they must confess the real problem. There are certain unconscious processes in the individual, as a matter of fact, which make him or her involuntarily shy away from the delicate area of difficulty. This means that skill is required on the part of the counselor to perceive the real problem underneath the irrelevant statements. The common practice of letting the counselee begin anywhere is sound, but the counselor then must open the way for the counselee to talk about the real problem.

For the period of the confession, the counselor must be *incapable of being shocked or offended*. There was nothing in the above case to offend; but in most cases, if one goes deeply enough, there comes to light material the mere hearing of which would shock many persons. But the counselor who is shocked or offended forfeits the right at that moment to be a counselor—such a reaction is a sign that the counselor's own ego has insinuated itself into the picture. Being offended is, in fact, a way of withdrawing and protecting oneself. Someone who is shocked by the use of certain sex words, or the description of certain sex practices, cannot qualify as a counselor in these areas. This is particularly important because many counselees will attempt, consciously or unconsciously, to shock the listener. That is one expression of their neurosis. And if the listener is shocked, the counselee's neurosis becomes all the worse, and the value of the interview is destroyed. Calm objectivity, which is based on the realization that nothing which is human is foreign or unworthy of understanding, is the attitude for the counselor.

Emotional upsets during the confession period are sometimes a relief to the counselee and sometimes resistances. To have the counselee crying on one's shoulder is often a sign not so much of the success of the counselor as confidant but of the mismanagement of the interview. There is a tendency for counselees to become emotionally upset, they are expressing ideas and fears and suppressed material which they have possibly never told to anyone else. Many of them break down and cry. Here is where the counselor must exercise skill by remaining calm and making sure this calm carries, by means of empathy, into the counselee. Sometimes it may be advisable to let the counselee cry a little, but as soon as the tension has been released, the counselor will bring the counselee back again to emotional equilibrium. This is why the counselor should be wary about giving out sympathy in the interview; sympathy, when it is personal and subjective, can augment the emotional upsets. Empathy is the better attitude because it is objective and includes all that is valuable of sympathy. Its importance cannot be overestimated, for in empathy lies the secret of controlling the mood of the interview.

Turning now to the interpretation stage of the interview, we find several important guides for counselors. First, *interpretation is a function of the counselor and counselee working together*. It is not a case of the counselor's figuring out the pattern and then presenting it on a platter to the other.

This brings us to the more specific point: the counselor *suggests interpretations* rather than stating them dogmatically. He or she does not say, "This is this," but rather, "This *appears* to be this," or "This is *connected* with this"; and waits to see how the counselee reacts to the suggestion. As we have stated previously, all conclusions in personality matters are of the nature of hypotheses; and the truth of the hypothesis is contingent upon the way it works in the personality at hand.

This leads to a third observation: the counselor must be able *to read the meaning of the counselee's reactions to suggestions*. If the counselee accepts the counselor's suggested interpretation, as Bronson so often did, by saying calmly, "Yes, I think that is true," the suggestion may be accepted by both for the time being. But if the counselee is quite indifferent, the suggestion not seeming to make any difference, the counselor discards the idea, concluding he or she has not yet struck anything very significant. If the counselee rejects the suggestion violently, protesting vehemently that it is untrue, the counselor may tentatively conclude that the suggestion *is* probably the correct interpretation and has struck close to the root of the problem. But the counselor must never insist at the time, but merely retreats, takes another lead, and from this new angle approaches the same center of the problem. If the counselor is successful in hitting upon the true interpretation, he or she will find the counselee giving up resistance and admitting the truth even of the originally rejected suggestion.

3
Limitations of Counseling

We shall conclude this section with a word on the limitations of the counselor's technique. The counselor cannot expect to uncover the total personality pattern of the individual; it is not, in fact, his or her province to do so. His function, rather, is first to listen objectively and thus help the counselee confess and "air" aspects of the problem; second, to aid the counselee to understand the deeper sources of the personality from which the problem arises; and third, to point out relationships which will give the counselee a new understanding of himself or herself and equip the counselee thereby to solve the problem. The less experienced the counselor is, the more should the counselor's function be confined to the confession stage, with interpretation suggested only tentatively. But upon becoming more experienced, he or she is increasingly able to offer fruitful interpretations which will help disclose the deeper relationships in the personality pattern.

Tests and questionnaires and other standardized forms for obtaining basic information about personalities can be useful if employed with discretion. A counselor in a college situation can often obtain suitable forms, such as vocational aptitude tests and personal prejudice tests, from the psychology or sociology departments of the institution. Oftentimes the college authorities are willing to cooperate to the extent of making available to the counselor the intelligence quotient of the student as shown in the entrance examination. The counselor will probably end up working out a questionnaire for obtaining personality information. This should include the basic items we have suggested previously, such as family and background, age, matters like physical health, hobbies, special interests, and friendships.

It is advisable for the counselor to keep some notation of the various facts in the case, if only to assure objectivity and to restrain his or her wishful thinking. My practice has been to jot down the essential facts while the counselee is talking in the confession stage, always however, requesting permission beforehand and assuring the counselee the notes will be destroyed if he or she desires at the conclusion of the counseling series. This notation gives a professional and businesslike touch to the interview. It is a way of keeping all aspects of the picture before one. Still another value is that the counselor is then afforded an opportunity to study the facts between consultations and possibly gain some new insights into the counselee's personality pattern. After casual moments of contact with a counselee such as on hikes or chance walks, I may jot down the significant facts about someone I am seeing as background for my future contacts.

How many periods of consultation should the counselor plan to hold in a given case? This varies, of course. Some times one consultation is all that is practicable. But in every case where it is desired to penetrate somewhat deeply into the personality pattern in instances, for example, of distinct personality difficulties, it is advisable to plan arbitrarily for a series of interviews. The plan I customarily follow consists of six interviews lasting one hour each, spaced at two a week. An appointment is made for a definite hour, rather than leaving it simply as a matter of "dropping in next week." This period of three weeks gives both parties—particularly the counselee—time to reflect on the insights discovered in each successive interview; and by reason of the assimilative and selective processes of unconsciousness, the counseling takes up at a deeper level each time.

Long periods of consultation are not to be recommended. Occasionally student counselors tell of three- and four-hour interviews of an evening; but such affairs are usually connected with emotional strain, which befuddles the counseling. After a certain period, both counselor and counselee lose the power to be objective, and subjective attitudes are bound to creep in. Ordinarily, we may conclude, one hour is an optimum duration for an interview.

VII   *The Transforming of Personality*

We now consider the final stage in the counseling procedure, the consummation and goal of the whole process—the transforming of the counselee's personality. In the confession and interpretation stages we found that the source of his or her problem was a faulty adjustment of tensions within the personality. This maladjustment, it was observed, went hand in hand with mistaken attitudes toward life. The wrong attitudes need to be corrected as far as possible, and need thus some readjustment of the tensions effected. This is called "transforming" because it does give the personality a new "form"; it changes, not necessarily the content, but certainly the structure; it is a readjustment of the constellation of tensions which constitutes the form of the personality.

In the counseling process we do not remold the individual completely into a new person. The endeavor is to free the counselee to be himself or herself. This means giving the counselee the start in the task of transforming personality.

And how is this to be done?

1
Limits of Advice

In the first place, *personality is not transformed by advice*. This misconception we must destroy once and for all; true counseling and the giving of advice are distinctly different functions. Sometimes, of course, everyone is put in the role of adviser: the dean must advise the new student about certain courses of which the student as yet knows nothing, or one must advise the stranger which bus to take downtown. But in neither of these cases is the personality of the individual being dealt with. No deep understanding, and very little empathy, enters into the process. Advice (using the term in its everyday sense) is always superficial; it is a handing down of directions from above, a one-way traffic. True counseling operates in a deeper sphere, and its conclusions are always the product of two personalities working together on the same level.

The psychotherapists do not mince words in their rejection of the position of adviser. Many quotations could be cited of the same tenor as the following one from Freud: "Moreover, I assure you that you are misinformed if you assume that advice and guidance in the affairs of life is an integral part of the analytic influence. On the contrary, we reject this role of the mentor as far as possible. Above all, we wish to attain independent decisions on the part of the patient."[1]

Advice giving is not an adequate counseling function because it violates the autonomy of personality. It has been agreed that personality must be free and autonomous; how, then, can one person justifiably pass ready-made decisions down to another? Ethically one cannot do it; and practically one cannot—for advice from above can never effect any real change in the other's personality. The idea never becomes part of the counselee, who will cast it off at the earliest convenience. The old adage is still fitting, "Advice can be had for nothing, and is usually worth it." Practically speaking, however, counselors are called on to give advice in matters that are not strictly personality problems. Here one may do so, but let it be clear that one is not genuinely counseling at that moment.

Sometimes advice may work legitimately as suggestion, the individual thus remaking the decision for himself or herself. But this represents a different process, which we shall consider below. The important consideration is that every decision of account must come, in the end, from the counselee. "In my view," Rank aptly says, "the patient should make himself what he is, should will it and do it himself, without force or justification and without need to shift the responsibility for it."[2]

2
The Leaven of Suggestion

Turning now to the positive means of transforming personality, let us first consider the *leaven of suggestion*. Suggestion is often condemned as a technique in personality influence, but that is due to a misconception; rightly understood, suggestion is seen to play an inescapable role in all personal development. Every individual is continually receiving suggestions of every sort from the environment. The pertinent question is, why accept certain suggestions and reject others? The answer lies in the nature of his or her personality pattern. It is not accurate to attribute the downfall of an individual to the suggestion of someone in the environment, or to a book, or to anything else external. We must ask, what was there in this individual's personality pattern which would permit him or her to accept the suggestions from outside?

Every individual has tendencies toward many different forms of behavior. We can think of each person's unconscious as throbbing with a number of instinctive "pushes" knocking for expression in the outside world. To use Plato's time-honored figure, there are in the unconscious a number of horses straining at the bit to be off in different directions. In the healthy individual, the conscious ego selects the direction of which it approves, and restrains the other tendencies. Neurosis means a weakening of the ego's guidance, an inability to decide in which direction the movement should be made, and hence a crippling of effective action. Now a suggestion from the environment may be the touch needed to loosen one of these tendencies which is already strong within the individual.

3
Citing Constructive Alternatives

The counselor cannot escape using suggestion in some form, so he or she may as well be intelligent about using it. During counseling he or she may throw out a number of suggestions as a fisherman does certain kinds of flies, waiting to see what fly the trout will leap to catch. Many of the suggestions will appear to have no effect; but others will suddenly be seized by the counselee, will be accepted into his or her mind and there loosened to work like a leaven. The suggestion of the counselor here becomes coupled with a tendency already in the unconscious, and the combination may be enough to bring the counselee to a decision. In this case, the counselee has been enabled to draw into expression some new phase of the unconscious, and moves forward with the self more unified.

In some cases, therefore, the most useful function of the counselor is *to lay all the constructive alternatives before the counselee*. From these alternatives the counselee's unconscious selective process will choose what it needs.

It is the purpose of a book like this, for example, to throw out numerous suggestions in somewhat organized form on the subject of counseling, not with the hope—heaven forbid!—that anyone use the book like a mathematics table, but rather with the expectation that the suggestions will combine creatively with the tendencies already in the reader's mind and thus give birth to an understanding of counseling that will be uniquely the brain-child of the reader.

The second factor in the transforming of personality is the *creative function of understanding*. This is to say, brusquely, that in the very understanding of the problem some transformation in the personality of the counselee takes place. It is the basic assumption of Adlerian therapy that if the patient understands truly he or she will act rightly, the modern development of the old Socratic maxim "Knowing is doing." Certainly there is basic truth in this contention that knowledge leads to virtue; it is an assumption which is made to some degree by all psychotherapy. Knowing the truth *does* imply some compulsion to do the truth; if it be really true, one's happiness and future welfare depend upon doing it. I pointed out above that neurotic forms of behavior are forms of self-deceit, and that if this deceit be unmasked— i.e., the rationalization and false motives removed—the ego will be forced to relax its self-defeating training formula and direct itself into socially constructive forms of behavior.

In the stage of interpretation, the counselor automatically employs this method of transforming character, in attempting to give the counselee understanding of the factors which have led to difficulties. In this very understanding a creative activity will automatically be set in motion in the counselee's mind to correct the mistakes.

We observed in the previous chapter how the creative function of understanding worked in the case of Bronson. As an epitomizing of the interpretation, the counselor suggested two specific questions to Bronson with the intention that these questions should work like searchlights in Bronson's mind in the future, continually pointing out to him new insights into his personality problem and thus aiding him toward clarification. Sure enough, Bronson returned a few days later to tell how he had suddenly awakened out of a fantasy as he was riding on the sub-way and discovered that he had been subconsciously pondering and worrying for fifteen minutes about how he was to find time to prepare his lectures. "This fits in with the attitude of insecurity which we found in my personality," he said. And in this instance he had simply laughed at how his old pattern was endeavoring to work him into a useless nervous tension as it had customarily done in the past—and his laughing served temporarily to relieve the tension. Thus, as this understanding more and more works in Bronson's mind, consciously, but even more unconsciously, he will move in geometric progression toward personality health.

But knowledge is not the whole of virtue, and understanding is not all one needs to transform personality. And so it is necessary to move on to further considerations.

The third means of transforming character is one implied in an earlier chapter, *the influence resulting from the empathetic relationship*. The two personalities being to an extent merged, influence must inevitably flow from the counselor to the counselee and vice versa. This means that the counselor affects some transfor-mation of the other's character merely by directing his or her own mood and willing during the empathetic relationship.

Rank points out that his method in therapy is to make it possi-ble for the patient to identify with the therapist's positive will, the patient thus taking on extra strength to triumph over his or her own negative will. Thereupon the patient learns to will positively and constructively. I assume this is very much the same process that we have been explaining in terms of empathy.

In counseling I make it a specific practice near the end of the interview to *will courage*, knowing that this courage will carry over into the will of the counselee. During the *confession* we have both become pessimistic, for the counselee's despair has carried into my mood; then in the *interpretation* we have progressed toward a clarified view of the situation; and as the solution to the problem and the new mode of behavior present themselves, courage has taken the place of the despair. I know that my courage, as counselor, will become the counselee's whether I make specific statements of courage or not, as our psychic states are to an extent identified. This willing courage may sound like send-

ing the counselee out with a "psychological boost"; but if it is
that, it is a "boost" which is a relatively deep function in
personality.

To give a simple illustration. A student at a formal tea is standing in the corner, shy and embarrassed and in general having
a poor time. As counselor you walk over with the intention of
helping him out of his negative mood. Suppose you try the
method of advice; you clap him on the shoulder and say enthusiastically, "Buck up, old man, smile and have a good time."
He then makes a feeble attempt to buck up, puts on a forced
smile, feels all the more guilty about his shyness, and so gets even
more embarrassed. His second state is worse than the first. Or
suppose you try the method of suggestion. You remark, "A lot
of interesting people here. This is a good chance to get to know
them." Now he has already thought that—at least thought that
he should be thinking it—and so the suggestion may do some
good. But the best method is the empathetic one. You first allow
your psychic states to become merged by taking on his mood,
and you may remark something to this effect, "Too bad these
teas have to be so formal. It's pretty hard to feel at home." The
shy boy brightens up and answers with genuine enthusiasm, "Yes,
it certainly is!" as this is exactly the idea that has been upper-
most in his mind. Empathy is achieved, but in achieving it you
have surrendered some of your own happiness to take on his
unhappiness. But after a moment's conversation you again
perceive the possibilities in the tea, and your optimism and
courage return. This time he takes on your mood, which over-
comes his shyness and embarrassment. And the conclusion of our
parable would be that he begins to move about the room with
courage and interest in the other people.

4
Utilizing Counselee's Suffering

The fourth factor in the transforming of character is the *utilization of suffering*. The counselor may channel the suffering of the

neurotic counselee to furnish the power to bring about the transformation of character.

A human being will not change his or her personality pattern, when all is said and done, until forced to do so by suffering. Advice, persuasion, requests from the outside will effect only a temporary change in the cloak of the personality. And here is where mere rational understanding is shown to be inadequate, for to bring about a real change it takes a dynamic stronger than simply an abstract idea that another way would be "better." The human ego is a recalcitrant and stubborn affair; it fights off disturbance, as it very much fears the profound insecurity that comes when its style of life is shaken. In fact, many neurotic individuals prefer to endure the misery of their present situation than to risk the uncertainty that would come with change. No matter how clearly the neurosis may be shown to be based on sheer falsehood, the patient will not give up until suffering becomes insupportable.

Fortunately the wheels of life do grind relentlessly on and bring a just portion of suffering as a penalty for every neurotic attitude. When this misery becomes so great that the individual is willing to give up a wrong attitude, in fact to give up everything, he or she has arrived at that state of desperation which is prerequisite for any cure at all. We can agree that this state of desperation is required; but since in counseling we deal ordinarily with minor cases of personality difficulty, the desperation may be limited to the area of the particular problem.

Fortunately every wrong attitude brings its suffering, but unfortunately most persons do not use this suffering constructively. The neurotic will turn this suffering back into a vicious circle. For example, the counselee, say a shy student, suffers from painful embarrassment at a college social function, and therefore resolves not to go to any more parties. This, of course, makes the problem all the worse. It is the function of the counselor to channel this suffering constructively, i.e., to connect it with the mistaken attitude. This will mean pointing out that the student's suffering is really due to egocentricity, a lack of social interest, at the party, and that staying away will be an expression of even greater egocentricity and therefore will make the suffering ultimately all the worse.

Suffering is one of the most potentially creative forces in nature. It is not sentimentality to relate the greatness of certain characters to their sufferings. As the pearl is produced in the endeavor of the oyster to adjust itself to the irritation of the grain of sand, so the great works of Poe and Shelley and Van Gogh and Dostoevski are understandable only in relation to the sufferings these artists experienced.

Jung expresses this truth: "But all creativeness in the realm of the spirits as well as every psychic advance of man arises from a state of mental suffering."[3] And the vicious circle of suffering may become constructive. "When we see that the pain is the first step toward being reborn, and that all that has happened, no matter how miserable, is only a necessary step toward clarification, no sorrow or torment, or even joy has been in vain."[4]

People should then rejoice in suffering, strange as it sounds, for this is the sign of the availability of energy to transform their characters. Suffering is nature's method of indicating a mistaken attitude or way of behavior, and to the objective and nonegocentric person every moment of suffering is the opportunity for growth. In this sense we can be "glad we're neurotic"—glad, that is, if we are able to utilize the suffering.

A counseling principle arises here: *the counselor should not relieve the counselee of suffering, but rather redirect the suffering into constructive channels*. The counselor should use this suffering like water power which, when rightly channeled, generates the dynamic capable of effecting the personality transformation.

The counselor should not assume the individual's final responsibility for working out his or her own salvation. In severe cases the counselor may assume some of the responsibility temporarily, but only to give it back in more definite form to the counselee in the end. This principle is the basis for the practice of guarding against any intimate social relationships with the counselee during the period—assuming this lasts for several weeks—of the counseling. In these social contacts, the counselee will be almost certain to involve the counselor in a web of responsibility, assuming unconsciously, for example, that the counselor likes the counselee too much to let him or her fail. And thus the counselee shifts some of the responsibility to the other's shoulders. Calm objectivity, rather, is the best attitude during the duration of the counseling period.

It is sometimes said that the counselee should always go out of the office happier than when he or she entered. But this may indicate that the counseling was merely reassuring an old style of life. The patting on the back may do the counselee definite harm and postpone the final overcoming of the difficulty. The counselee should ordinarily go out more *courageous* after the interview, but courageous with the painful realization that his or her personality must be transformed. If the counseling has been more than superficial, he or she will feel shaken and probably unhappy.

At the conclusion of the interview, the counselee may feel some deep anger (which he or she may not even be conscious of at the time) toward the counselor, this person who has pointed out uncomfortable truths which he or she has been struggling for years to keep hidden. But this anger will soon be redirected to the mistaken personality pattern, and the counselee will then be profoundly grateful for the counselor's help. This case is probably typical: in a conference recently the counselee and I unearthed some truths which she found very disagreeable. Consequently she exhibited a negative attitude toward me for several days after the interview. I noticed this, of course, and interpreted it as a possible indication that we had hit upon her basic problem. Surely enough, a half week later she came to me with apologies for her negative attitude (which, however, she assumed I had not observed!) and explained that she had accepted our diagnosis and was frankly facing the need to transform her personality.

Cases are often met in which the dynamic initiative to give up the neurotic pattern is absent. In the interpretation stage, the counselee may abstractly see the value of character transformation, but tell himself or herself "Not yet." Then the counselor in most cases can only wait, knowing that when life in its own good time has piled upon this individual the suffering egocentricity merits, the counselee will humbly make the change. Suffering in this case would be a boon.

On rare occasions the skilled counselor can bring the suffering of the other person to a head in anticipation of the crisis. Recently an individual with whose style of life I had become very familiar wrote me that he had grown completely discouraged, that he felt life was unfair to him, and that he contemplated dropping out of school and bumming west. And at the conclusion of the outburst he asked my counsel. In the answering letter I aimed specifically to bring his suffering to a head. I pointed out that his attitude was that of a pampered child and that his unhappiness was due to his self-pity and lack of courage to manage his situation. I intentionally left no loophole in the letter for his ego prestige. For several weeks I did not hear from him, but when the answer did come, it was full of gratitude and assurances that my diagnosis had been correct and that he had already progressed far in overcoming the wrong attitudes.

This is not to be described as giving the individual a "jolt," or bringing him suffering he would otherwise have escaped. It is rather the drawing to a head of suffering that was potentially present, and thus averting a worse crisis. Needless to say, the counselor will not utilize this rather delicate method until having become quite skilled.

The counselor's function, to summarize, is to connect the individual's suffering with the neurotic aspects of his or her personality pattern. Dealing with an individual over a period of time, the counselor can point out each week the way the sufferings of the individual during the past week were related to mistaken attitudes and behavior. The counselor can even predict suffering, pointing out to the counselee that the next time he or she suffers from embarrassment at a social function or from quarreling with the family, it will be due to such and such a personality factor. Thus the grinding of nature's relentless wheels will be made to serve for good.

Finally, after all our discussion, we come to the realization that there is a great area in the transformation of personality which we do not understand, and which we can attribute only to *the mysterious creativity of life*. This lad has come in with a hangdog expression, timid, shy, feeling inferior at every turn—he appears defeated in the game of life before getting well started. But somehow the chrysalis of his narrow-self-concern is broken; he is transferred to the objective, expansive, and constructive side of life. His despair has given birth to hope, his selfishness has been replaced by unselfishness, his cowardice has changed to courage, his pain is outshone by joy, and his loneliness is being vanquished by love. In this transformation of personality we, as counselors, may have had some small thing to do. We know we have done precious little—merely guided a bit here, directed a bit there; and the creative forces of life have effected the miracle of transformation.

As the motto has it, "The physician furnishes the conditions—the Infinite works the cure."[5] Like the doctor, we may bind up the wound; but there are all the forces of life welling up in their incalculable spontaneity in the growing together of skin and nerve tissues and the reflowing of blood to perform the healing. Before the creative forces of life, the true counselor stands humbly. And this humility is not of the false sort; the deeper a counselor's understanding of personality, the more clearly the counselor realizes how minute his or her efforts in comparison to the greatness of the whole.

"It's here [a lunatic asylum] that men are most themselves—
themselves and nothing but themselves—sailing with outspread sails
of self. Each shuts himself in a cask of self, the cask stopped with a bung
of self and seasoned in a well of self. None has a tear for others' woes
or cares what any other thinks. . . .
"Now surely you'll say that he's himself! He's full of himself and
nothing else; himself in every word he says—himself when he's
beside himself. . . .
"Long live the Emperor of Self!"
HENRIK IBSEN, *Peer Gynt*,
ACT IV, SCENE 13

"Whosoever shall seek to gain his life shall lose it:
but whosoever shall lose his life shall preserve it."
LUKE 17: 33

PART

THREE

Ultimate
Considerations

VIII

The Personality of the Counselor

THE PERSONAL EQUATION is all important in counseling, as counselors can work only through themselves. It is therefore essential that this self be an effective instrument. All the therapists, and certainly the arguments of this book, would support Adler's statement, "The technique of treatment must be in yourself."

1

What Makes a Good Counselor?

The superficial qualities of the good counselor are self-evident:

winsomeness, the ability to be at ease in other people's company, a capacity to empathize, and other characteristics which may be equally ambitious in meaning. These qualities are not wholly innate but also can be acquired to a great extent. Their development comes as a consequence of the counselor's own clarification and his and her interest and enjoyment of other people. To put it bluntly, if the counselor genuinely enjoys the company of others and wishes them well, he or she finds himself or herself automatically being the kind of person that attracts them. So often we find that the person who is not liked is the one who unconsciously does not want to be liked, either because of what other people's affections would require or because of the wish for solitariness. "Personal attractiveness" is a term often used but exasperatingly seldom defined; we can now define it as *the reverse side of one's own interest in and enjoyment of other persons*.

But to penetrate more deeply into the problem, what differentiates a good counselor from a poor one? Is it training? Some training would appear necessary, but it is easy to see that prolonged graduate work in experimental psychology as it is at present taught would not necessarily fit one for effective counseling—and might even unfit one. Freud expressed our answer classically when, in pointing out that medical training is not necessary as a prerequisite for the psychoanalyst, he stated that the quality which is essential is "inherent insight into the human soul—first of all into the unconscious layers of his own soul—and practical training."[1]

Freud thus gives us the clue. This "practical training" means the ability to escape from the tendency to counsel on the basis of one's own more or less rigid prejudices. This ego bias is so stubborn a hydra-headed monster that one must exercise all one's ingenuity in overcoming it. The case of a student, for example, who had shifted around among many professional schools and finally ended up in a theological seminary, was presented to a seminar I held with a group of persons in religious vocations. There was the immediate consensus in the group that, although the young man unfortunately had vacillated, he had at last found his right niche! If the group had been one of doctors, and the student had at last found his way into a medical school, the approval would have been as evident. Seeing others through one's own prejudices—this ego bias is clearly the worst stumbling block in the personality of the counselor.

How is the ego bias to be avoided? It cannot be eradicated entirely, but it can be understood and guarded against. For this reason the various schools of psychotherapy insist that the applicants for their field first be analyzed themselves in order to understand and remove as many as possible of their own complexes. If they were not, it is certain they would unconsciously be unable to avoid treating patients in terms of these complexes.

It would unquestionably be wise for the counselor to be analyzed by a professional psychotherapist. This discussion of his or her own personality with another could provide a priceless understanding of self and hence aid greatly in effectively counseling others. This does not mean that the would-be counselor would be taken apart piece by piece by the psychotherapist; treatment of one's self is rather a matter of the therapist's assisting the person better to understand his or her self. The right choice of a therapist is, of course, important. One can predict that in future generations some didactic therapy will be considered a requisite part of the training of teachers, ministers, and social workers.

Some would-be counselors will not be in a geographical position for sustained consultations with a psychotherapist. The next best way is the way pursued by Freud himself, namely, to analyze one's self. One gets the impression in reading Freud that he was fascinated by what turned up as he pierced into his own subconscious and his own dreams. The reader feels that Freud saw his own problems with the wonder with which the first Spaniards gazed upon the Pacific:

> "Then felt I like some
>   watcher of the skies
> When a new planet
>   swims into his ken,

. . .
Or like Cortez when with
    eagle eyes
He stared at the Pacific—
    and all his men
Looked at each other
    with a wild surmise—
Silent, upon a peak
    in Darien.''*

Freud arrived at many, if not most, of his basic insights—such
as the Oedipus pattern—through his own self-analysis. I, for one,
almost never go to sleep without a pencil and pad beside my bed
in order to catch whatever treasures of dreams I may have during
the night.

It is never possible to understand one's self completely—our
egos are too clever to be tracked down in their inmost lair without
outside assistance. But one can go a long way toward understanding one's self, and this will suit the immediate needs of many
counselors. It is my hope that this book, together with other books
in the field, will help the reader to gain an adequate understanding of himself or herself. When the counselor has conscientiously
gone as far as one can in analyzing one's self, it is helpful occasionally to have even a few sessions with a psychotherapist or
another counselor to help one see the particular quirks by which
one's ego deceives one's self.

2
Analysis of a Typical Counselor

To help readers in this task of understanding themselves, I shall
present an analysis of some ideas about counselors in general.

---

*From Keats, ''On First Looking Into Chapman's Homer.'' It does not matter that
the first Spaniard to see the Pacific was not Cortez but Vasco de Balboa.

This is a boiling down of the characteristics I have found recurring in a number of persons who have consulted with me, and it should, I hope, result in some sort of picture of the "typical neurosis" of people in this field.* After presenting this picture at a conference, I was accosted by several persons in the group with an insistent, "That was I," or "You were really talking about me, weren't you?" Of course, I had the pleasure of assuring them that it was no one in particular, and that if the shoe fitted them, I must have succeeded in my task of catching typical neurotic characteristics toward which such counselors tend. It is my hope that many readers will see themselves in the following analysis to a great enough extent to derive help in understanding their own patterns.

What characteristics do we observe in these typical religious workers? First, they work hard and conscientiously. They appear not to relax as often as people in other vocations, and do not have as many avocational interests. They are apt to throw themselves entirely into their jobs, taking conscious pride in this fact. They work at a tension, and in fact tend to carry this tension through twenty-four hours of the day, as their jobs are such as not to be limited by working hours. Sometimes this tension becomes so great that they find it difficult to take vacations or holidays without feelings of guilt.

These typical counselors carry responsibility well. They are careful about details in social as well as vocational matters—in fact, so careful of details as sometimes to irritate other people. We observe a great desire not to fail. The dread of failure, though normal when connected with important matters, is here exaggerated and connected with minor, unimportant things.

All of these observations point to the fact that the religious workers follow what Otto Rank called the "all or none" law, throwing themselves headlong into whatever they do with a lack of ability to respond partially. This lack of ability to partialize is connected with a lack of interests and friends outside work,

---

*This fictitious counselee happens to be a religious worker. This choice has something to do with my first experience, as Director of Men Students at Michigan State University, where my office was in an Interdenominal Peoples' Church.

the failure to enjoy the means of life but a preoccupation with absolute ends. One of the chief characteristics of neurotic individuals, incidentally, is a tendency toward complete concern with goals which become absolute and rigid in their minds.

Where there is great tension, a fear of failure in small things, and an unusually great concern for details, we suspect that strong ambition is present also. Surely enough, typical religious workers do possess an exaggerated ambition. They are particularly convinced of the indispensability and importance of their work, and we see them hurrying about here and there as though the world depended on it.

A normal conviction of the importance of one's work is healthy and desirable. But when it is expressed in a lasting tension in the worker, we can conclude that his or her ego pattern has become too much involved in the job. It is *his* or *her* vocation, and because of an exaggerated feeling of his or her own importance, the job must automatically be the world's most important. That is why people remark about such individuals, "They take themselves too seriously." This expresses almost the same overevaluation of one's self. A certain degree of ambition is healthy—the nonegocentric form, which is a spontaneous expression of the individual's creative abilities. But when the individual works with never-relaxing tension, we become suspicious that the motive is ego striving rather than the unselfish desire to contribute to humanity.

We might call this exaggerated ambition the "Messiah complex." It is one's conviction of the indispensability of one's own person, and the consequent feeling that one's particular work is indispensable to humanity and the universe. Thus, one is given a mask for pride and one sets oneself up as a reformer, a moral judge over one's fellows, and proceeds to speak *ex cathedra*. Granted that there may be no more important work in the world than helping people, that does not mean that it could not go on without one.

We have only to glance through history to see how dangerous this Messiah complex can become. How many a terrible inquisition was given demonic power by the fact that its progenitors persuaded themselves that they were doing Christ's will! This becomes an excuse for the waiving of the last vestiges of conscience and humane feeling; and the self-styled "holy man" who is using his holy vocation as a cloak for his own ego striving is more demonic (witness the crusaders in Constantinople) than a purely secular person. It is needless to add that the fact that this ego motive behind the Messiah complex is unconscious only makes the point the truer. In the typical religious worker, the process is unconscious, and it requires an objective point of view to determine how selfish is the motivation behind the zeal. The prestige of the Infinite used as the camouflage for one's own desire for domination—how ironically tragic that religion can be so misused![2]

It is also often observable that this typical religious worker has not solved the problem of sexual adjustment with particular success. Some persons in religious vocations appear not to feel the normal attraction for members of the opposite sex; but this apparent quiescence of the sexual urges may be evidence of a misdirection which may result in the impulses appearing later in more troublesome form. The tendency to rule out the sex function itself, as exhibited in the endeavor to think of marriage chiefly in terms of having a home and children, often indicates that the sex problem has not been honestly confronted.

One could have predicted what happened in the sexual scandals of Jimmy Swaggart and Jim Bakker, as persons who cry out so fervently, shouting from the housetops their righteousness, will get into the same scandals they so fervently preach against. In Sinclair Lewis' novel *Elmer Gantry*, he truthfully describes this process of superrighteousness and subsequent debacle. Aimie Semple McPherson in Lewis' day was the heroine preacher who shouted out powerfully against evil, and fell into her own hypocritical trap.

We can partly understand this failure to meet the sex problem as a product of our culture, which obviously is in the process of radically changing sexual behavior. We see on the one hand a great release from inhibition, but on the other hand a failure to take the dynamics of sex and procreation seriously.

Sometimes religious and other counselors use the concept of

"sublimation" as a rationalization for their failure to make an adequate endeavor to solve sexual problems. But sublimation, curious Freudian term that it is, does not have the meaning popularly given it in religious circles. Freud was endeavoring, when he employed this term, to explain social and artistic activities as one aspect of libido expression; he certainly did not mean that one can plunge into art or social service and thereby be totally relieved of sexual impulses. It is possible, of course, for one to reduce the tension in one's whole organism by work and exercise and enthusiastic participation in the not specifically sexual aspects of social activity—and to this limited extent, the popular meaning given the term "sublimation" is accurate. But we still have the normal sexual urge. We may well come to grips with the necessity of sexual deprivation if that is the situation, as it is with many priests and nuns who do deprive themselves without noticeable damage.

Of course, it is possible to live well without specific sexual expression, but the means of doing so is an honest and frank facing of the situation, not repression. The attempt to ignore and cover up the sex factor is, in most cases, clear dishonesty, and actually amounts to a "submerging" of the urge rather than sublimation. For people who find themselves in positions where sexual deprivation is necessary, the courageous and psychologically healthy adjustment is to admit the deprivation and frankly make the renunciation that is necessary. Even married persons must face this aspect of their lives with some ability for renunciation in specific situations. And the unmarried person who faces the problem honestly, escaping into neither repression nor libertinism, but exercising the courage to bear the necessary tensions, will be in the best position eventually to solve the love and marriage problem satisfactorily.

What are the results of the failure to come to terms with this problem in the work of counselors? First, they are clearly unfitted to advise others in the area of sex. The counselor must be on guard against forcing his or her own maladjustments upon others; if one's own sex problem is inadequately handled, one must step cautiously in that area in counseling others.

In the second place, the counselor with an unsolved sex problem may make emotional attachments which are harmful to the persons with whom he or she works. This is particularly true if the individual is specifically trying to "sublimate" in these other persons. We could cite the actual case of a women's student worker who thinks of the students part of the time as her children (this is conscious) and part of the time as her sweethearts (this, of course, is unconscious but evident to any intelligent observer). Such defenses introduce a subjective element which makes effective counseling difficult, if not impossible. One of the counselor's hardest tasks is to keep the counselee from becoming too attached to him or her; transference of feelings is a powerful reality. If the readiness for emotional attachment is present on the counselor's side as well, the counseling relationship needs to be handled with special care. Whenever the counselor finds himself or herself taking very special pleasure in the presence of the counselee's person, he or she had better look to his or her own motives.

To return to the deeper aspects of the personality of the typical religious worker: can we discover any pattern by which the whole style of life can be understood? We have pointed out that this individual throws himself or herself completely into work according to the "all or none" law, is especially careful of details, is apt to shelve the sex problem as separate from normal life, and exhibits an exaggerated opinion of the importance of the work.

The great care for details—and other symptoms here point in the same direction—is one of the telltale marks of what is termed the "compulsion neurosis." Sometimes called "obsessional neurosis," this is the neurosis of the person who for some inexplicable reason feels compelled to perform certain detailed forms of behavior that normally are not regarded as important. Going back every morning to try the door again though one knows one has locked it is an example of a harmless, and more or less universal, form of the neurosis. The person who is ridden by duty, particularly when this duty is a matter of external details, is another example. This compulsion neurosis is the typical neurosis of religious people, even the typical one of our day, according to Otto Rank. It is often connected with premonitions of spiritual or magical punishment. The severe compulsion neurotic feels, in some cases, that something supernaturally terrible will happen if he or she does not step on every crack in the sidewalk or tap every fencepost with a stick.

We saw in our typical male religious worker indications that he must not fail in details. He may believe that to ward off doom he must dress just right or pray in a special manner, as with the ancient pagan prayer wheels, or go through certain routines at his office. Why is he so afraid of failing? People fail at all times, as a matter of fact, even in big things, let alone in small matters. To err is human, but this individual has a peculiarly strong feeling that his mistakes will bring him magical doom.

It is a basic principle that neurotic ambition is connected with some deeper sense of inferiority; and, to be sure, we do find evidence in our typical religious worker of this inferiority feeling. It may take a moral form, with the individual experiencing unusual moral guilt and therefore making strenuous efforts to compensate by ambitious striving.

No matter what the sources of the inferiority, the consequent exaggerated ambition will, in this religious person, take a moral form. He will exhibit a "drive to be on top" morally. And he will feel special guilt when he is not on top. The "holier-than-thou" attitude is not an exception; it is merely the superiority complex, which is the reverse side of the inferiority feeling. The outsider can point out that the details do not make so much difference, but to this individual they do make a difference—all the difference of the ego supremacy, which is the central concern of life. Moral reformers—when their reforms do not have objective background—are to be understood in this category.

It is easy to see how some individuals can elevate themselves over other people by this technique of emphasizing petty moral and religious details. Indeed, in the case of the minister who gave up tea, coffee, and cocoa,* we see that the real reason was to make himself superior to persons around him who did indulge

---

*Discussed in final chapter.

in the beverages. Adler discusses such a case and concludes, "It illustrates how ambition breaks into religious problems, and how vanity makes its bearer a judge over virtue, vice, purity, corruption, good and evil."*

There is a more serious aspect to this problem, an aspect more arresting to those religiously sophisticated persons who do not fit into the above categories. It is this: religious persons, to the extent that they feel inferiority and a consequent exaggerated ambition, cannot refrain from morally judging other people. Since their ego strivings are in the moral realm, the depreciating of others morally will mean the elevating of themselves. No matter how often one rebukes oneself with the commandment, "Judge not," and no matter how viciously one suppresses these judgments, even deriving a certain pleasure from the refusal to "gossip," one will continue to condemn unconsciously. And unconscious judgment and condemnation of others are even more destructive than conscious judgment, so that we can prefer the overt expression of an individual's opinions of another if we know he or she has these opinions anyway. Is there no escape from the vicious circle? It is only through the understanding of the ego pattern—such as we are trying to do here.

This brings us to the matter of moral judgments in counseling. It is clear, first from a moral point of view, that no one has a right to judge another human being: the command "Judge not" is incontrovertible in the moral area. And psychotherapeutically, in the second place, judging is unpermissible: "And above all," as Adler says, "let us never allow ourselves to make any *moral* judgments concerning the moral worth of a human being!"[3]

But, as pointed out above, it is precisely the religious counselor who finds it most difficult not to condemn. Jung remarks that the reason people hesitate to confess to their minister but go to a psychiatrist instead is their fear that the minister will condemn. "He is never in touch when he passes judgment . . . we can get in touch with another person only by an attitude of unprejudiced objectivity."[4] Some Freudians, therefore, contend that the therapist should be ethically neutral, which cuts religious people out. This does not solve the problem, however. No therapist can be ethically neutral; such is one of the delusions of some branches of Freudianism. The therapist—in our case, the counselor—must presuppose some kind of ethical meaning, and he or she who refuses to do so consciously is still doing so unconsciously.

The only way out is for the counselor to learn to esteem and appreciate other persons without condemning them. It is the way of understanding, of "unprejudiced objectivity," the way of empathy, as we have seen in an earlier chapter. The ability to "judge not" is the watershed between authentic religion and egocentric religiosity.

After discussing at length these typical neurotic tendencies of religious workers, let us conclude with suggestions on how to overcome them, and thereby the fitting of the counselor for effective service.

In the first place, the counselor must understand the particular form this neurotic pattern takes in his or her own personality. The very understanding will go far toward clarification, and certainly it will illuminate the quirks in one's self against which one must guard when counseling others. In understanding one's inferiority feeling, one will see one's selfish ambition in its naked form, and so the neurotic aspect of one's ambition should become relaxed. Let no one think that this relaxing will diminish a person's productivity and creativity. It will, in fact, increase one's creative insights—as creativity requires the spontaneity which comes from periodic relaxation, and is blocked by the tension of strong ego striving.

3
The Courage of Imperfection

In the second place, the counselor needs to develop what Adler called the *courage of imperfection*. This means the ability to fail.

The compulsive neurotic who is not willing to fail must fight only on minor battlefields; no wonder such persons concern themselves with details, as in their own little backyards they do not risk failure. The courage of imperfection means the transferring of one's efforts to a major battlefield where significant things are done and failure or success becomes relatively incidental.

In the third place, the counselor needs to learn to *enjoy the process* of living as well as the goals. This will enable us to escape the "all or none" compulsion: enjoying the process means deriving enjoyment "on the wing" as one moves toward ends. And this enjoying of the process will relieve us of the necessity of having ulterior motives for our actions, doing this or that for the sake of some end which is outside the picture.

In the fourth place, let the counselor be sure he or she is *interested in people for their own sakes*. If one still believes one loves them "for God's sake," let one ask whether this "God" is not a covering for one's own ego striving. Is this cliché an excuse for a failure to appreciate persons for and in themselves?

This means that would-be counselors will have to do some genuine purging of themselves, relentlessly ferreting out the false elements and expurgating them by the classical method of repentance. When we can do this, it will be proved that the dedicated approach cuts the Gordian knot of the ego bias in counseling, and that, in the end, the truly devoted person makes the best counselor.

IX

Morals and Counseling

EVERY PERSONALITY PROBLEM is, in one sense, a moral problem, as it refers to that question which is basic to all ethics, "How shall I live?" We can expect that the creative personality will be distinguished by the ability to negotiate the moral relations of life adequately, and we can set it down as a basic principle that a constructive moral adjustment to life is the aim of successful counseling.

The mistake made by many inexperienced counselors is in attempting to take a shortcut to this goal, jumping too quickly to the moral implications of the problem. Then they endeavor, often without realizing it, to advocate to the counselee a specific set of moral standards. Now it is to be granted that the counselee may need moral standards, and granted also that the counselor will possess more or less adequate standards of his or her own which could be passed on. But in actual practice such a procedure short-circuits that counseling process and robs counselees of their inalienable right to mold their own morality in the crucible of their own struggles and aims in life.

Let us observe what happens when the counselor makes this mistake and approaches the interview from a moralistic point of view. A minister recently described to me the case of a student who had come to him with the problem of compulsive masturbation. In counseling with this student, the minister had pictured to him his future love relationship, marriage, and home, and had then exhorted him to keep these ideals before him and thus conquer the temptation to masturbate.

What happens? The student goes home, let us say, to his solitary room where he lives in somewhat lonely fashion (it is often solitary and lonely persons who are troubled with this problem), and there he will fight the urge to masturbate by holding up before himself the image of his future home. But this image is important to him at the time only because it has become connected, through the minister's exhortation, with his temptation. And so the more he thinks of the so-called ideal, the more vividly the idea of masturbation arises in his mind. Furthermore, the minister's exhortation has probably increased his guilt feeling, and consequently he hates himself and struggles against himself the more bitterly. Now the desire to masturbate has become stronger in this process, in fact stronger every moment he had held the idea in his mind even in the attempt to vanquish it. At the same time, his esteem of himself has been lowered as his guilt feelings have increased. Eventually he concludes that if he is such a depraved creature anyway he might as well give in to the urge. A vicious circle has been set up that makes the problem of the young man all the worse.

One is surprised that the simple psychology of temptation is not better understood in our day. It is clear, even without profound psychological understanding, that most temptations are not to be conquered by a direct, frontal attack. This only emphasizes the temptation, and if it be a matter of desire—such as liquor or sex—the more it is emphasized, the more vivid the desire becomes.

Constructively speaking, the best way to remove the power of temptation is to remove the image from the center of attention. To do this, the individual must become sufficiently interested in healthy pursuits that there is no attention left for the unhealthy desire. The adage has it that "an expulsive affection drives out temptations"; this is true to the extent that the affection is genuine and not merely seized upon with the ulterior purpose of using it as a weapon.

When all is said and done, the thing necessary is that the individual make a courageous, zestful, many-sided adjustment to living—and against this healthy personality, with all its enthusiastic interests, specific temptations will have little power. This is the approach that should have been taken in the above instance. If the minister had probed below the problem on the surface, he would no doubt have found that the masturbation was merely a symptom of some deeper personality maladjustment, and he could then have helped the student to a more healthy adjustment. Holding up the ideal of the future love and home is not in itself wrong; constructive goals do have an important function in counseling. But the goal, or ideal, must grow out of the situation, not be merely handed down from above. It must be indigenous to the counselee, an expression of his or her unique aims in line with the development of his or her unique personality.

By itself, either in preaching or in counseling, exhortation accomplishes very little good, and may do definite harm. It will increase the individual's guilt feeling and thus make him or her struggle harder but in a negative way. No doubt the student in the above example had been "trying" too hard already, as it is characteristic of persons with personality difficulties that they struggle hard but destructively. They are like fish caught in a net—the more desperately they struggle, the worse they become caught. Destructive struggling causes a greater disunity in the personality, and that is exactly what we wish to avoid. To use another figure, such an individual's will has become knotted up like two wrestlers who have such strong holds on each other that neither can move. No wonder the person cannot act effectively in the outside world!

We are not belittling *tension* or genuine *willing*, both of which are part of the healthy personality. But they must be based upon understanding. The willing then will not be a wrestling match merely on the surface of the person's mind but a reorganization of the whole personality for movement in the new direction.

For these reasons it is necessary to emphasize the principle that *the problem of the counselee should be approached as a matter of mental health, not of morality*. Then both counselor and counselee will be able to view it objectively, with a minimum of squeamishness or prudishness getting in the way. Putting aside superficial, immediate moralism, in the end they will be fitted to arrive closer to a true morality, which will endure.

1
Creative Individuality in Morals

Moral living, like all living, begins with people's self-expression—expression of their passions, their instinctual drives, their desires and inner urges of every sort. Morality means self-expression in terms of structure. However, the point to be emphasized is that without the individual's self-expression there can be no content to moral living. The instinctual drives of hunger and sex, the passions of anger and hate and love, the desires to make friends and to create—all of these urges and an infinite number of others furnish the material which is the content for morality. Without them there would be nothing to morality but a dry form like a river bed where no water flows.

We speak of these instinctual urges as surging up from the individual's unconsciousness. Freud has given us his unforgettable description of this "id," the seething cauldron out of the dark unconsciousness from which emerge all sorts of instinctual urges and appetites and desires. These are typified, in Freudian terms, by libido. And Jung, we recollect, carried through the description of the unconscious to include hopes and fears and images and every type of psychic content. Out of this reservoir come the fantasies which become the great art of humankind, the creative ideas which are the embryos of philosophies, and the insights which are developed into the ultimate concerns of religion.

The basic instinctual urge in each individual has been given different names by philosophers and psychologists: it is the "*elan vital*" or vital impulse of Bergson, the "will to power" of Nietzsche, or the "creative will" of Schopenhauer, and so on. Whatever the name, we are here dealing with the inner, irrational urges which give the content to human living. This is the creative flow, the stream of life which rises internally like an artesian well and pours out its living waters.

The content furnished by these instinctual urges is both good and evil. The "good" we define as instinctual urges which are directed in socially constructive ways. But by themselves the urges are more egocentric and antisocial than good. They are irrational and rebel against direction; they are like wild horses straining at the bit.

People are frightened by this instinctual side of their lives. They recognize something dangerous in the inner urges impelling them to love and to hate, to make sexual conquest and to fight, to seize the world in ambition and force themselves into ascendancy over other people. There is some of Faust in each of us—the urge to master the whole world, to express our will to live without limit—and it terrorizes us. In these powerful urges we sense tendencies toward destruction of ourselves as well as destruction of others.

Modern "civilized" people naturally hate to admit the existence of these urges, many of which are definitely antisocial and would create havoc in any community if allowed direct expression. We are chagrined to realize that we possess, and are possessed by, many more powerful irrational impulses than our self-respect would like; we are more the raging animal, in Freud's terms, than we would wish. And so we seek to repress the instinctual side of our personality. We prefer not to admit the instinctual urges into consciousness at all.

But that way out is denied, except by the detour of neurosis. Therefore, we take what appears to be the next best method, the endeavor to control our urges by superficial willing, by strengthening our superego and placing it like a powerful guard at the outlet of the id. Protestantism, in particular, has tended in this direction—tended, that is, to assume that the issues of life can be settled in the sphere of immediate, conscious decision. Thus we speak of "mastering life" and "conquering one's self." We sign a card or make a public statement and assume that the matter is settled.

After realizing that outright repression will not work, people tend to set up systems of rules by which they can control their instinctual urges. In adolescence especially we make lists of "rules for life." The more frightened we are of our urges, the more rigid these rules become. People may devise a detailed system of inflexible principles which they can apply in mechanical fashion to every situation. Adler speaks pointedly of these people who

> "attempt to pigeon-hole every activity and every event according to some principle which they have assumed valid for every situation . . . We have the impression that they feel themselves so insecure that they must squeeze all of life and living into a few rules and formulae, lest they become too frightened of it. Faced with a situation for which they have no rule or formulae, they can only run away."[1]

This rule making relieves such people of the difficult responsibility of making new decisions.

People are right in their fear of their instinctual urges. Therein lie dangerous potentialities for evil as well as great possibilities for creative good. Their mistake is in taking shortcuts; the techniques of repression, simple inhibition, and rule making simply

do not work. We cannot control these powerful forces in the unconscious by dishonesty. We may succeed in being respectable
and circumspect and never overstep the rules in the community,
but then we throw ourselves into a war which spreads hate and
murder over continents until whole countries are red with blood.
Or we may be perfectly moral in our own personal life but create
such poison in our surroundings by repressions that our children
are turned out into the world semineurotic.

Even in the case of the individual alone, it is clear that direct
"fighting" of the unconscious urges will not work. Here is John
Doe, for example, a man who attempts to guide himself by detailed rules and resolutions. He resolves this or that thing in his
conscious mind and then holds to the resolution with a tenacity,
which we unfortunately call "will power." But it is the forces
from deeper levels of unconsciousness which have most to do with
John Doe's or anybody else's behavior. And if his resolution is
made without reference to the "cauldron of the id," we can be
sure it will ultimately be "steam-rollered." Then Mr. Doe wonders
why, no matter how hard he consciously tries, he cannot keep
his resolutions! As a matter of fact, the very resolutions Mr. Doe
has made may incite a compensatory process in his unconscious,
which, when it finally bursts forth, will cause him to swing back
to the opposite extreme.

What we need is *cooperation* between the instinctual urges
and conscious aims. If there is mainly antagonism between id
and superego, the result is a greater and greater separation of
the conscious portion, and we find ourselves suddenly pushed
by God-knows-what powers in ourselves. No wonder our ancestors
believed in Satanic possession! The "devil" is much more powerful than nice people assume! The ideal situation is that the rider
(the conscious ego, in Freud's phrase) intelligently guides the
horses (the forces from the id). We can begin such a relationship
of cooperation only on the basis of understanding and reconcilia-
tion. It means that the individual must above all be *honest* with
his or her instinctual urges. Willing then will not be a private
wrestling match on the limited surface of consciousness, but a

reorganization of the whole person. Instead of merely *making resolutions*, one will *become resolved*. One's decisions, backed by forces from the "profound and powerful depths," will then have power and effectiveness.

All the good we have in life has its source in these instinctual urges, as does evil. Love springs up as well as hate, Eros as well as Thanatos. Sexuality has wrecked many a life, but it has also led to the creation of families, great loves, and great literature. The anger that surges up in us can be used to attack evils and result in great humanitarian reforms. So one who turns roughly against one's instinctual life may succeed temporarily in avoiding evil, but one has also blocked off one's possibilities for doing good. He who cannot hate, said Emerson, cannot love. Goethe's *Faust* not only created havoc in leading to the death of Gretchen, killing her brother by treachery, but he also built great dikes and houses so that the land could be cultivated. The individuals who try to dry up their instinctual urges rob their lives of content; their river is dry. So even if we could repress this dark and unruly side of our natures, we would not want to. We should have become rid of our chaff, but would find ourselves without any wheat.

Life is, therefore, a much more portentous affair than our little systems admit. We human beings are not the petty creatures our morality of mere "effort" implies. People can build great civilizations, and then wreck them with such violence that there is naught left but blood and smoldering ruins. Humans will let themselves be killed for love or hate, and they will kill others for the same reasons. We can let our personalities dissipate until we scarcely can be distinguished from the animals, yet we can develop our minds until our "thoughts go wandering through eternity," and we can loosen our creative fantasies until we make delicate Gothic spires that in sheer beauty rank with the creations of God. The world wars are our doing, but so is the culture of Classical Greece. For centuries we have marched in armies, but for as many centuries we have tilled the soil and watched the plants come up in the spring, and we fed our fellows with the fruits of the land.

Life is not a matter for simple optimism, for there is evil; nor for mere pessimism, for there is good. *The possibility for nobility in the face of evil is what gives life tragic meaning.*

Our attitude toward our instinctual urges should be, then, not one of conflict and repression but rather one of understanding and cooperation, aiming toward the utilization of these forces for good. This takes courage, as instincts and id are more powerful than we know; it means looking below the superficial and petty moral rules in the interests of a more meaningful morality.

2.
Structure in Morality

A counselor related to me the story of Janice, an attractive college woman who had become filled with a general dissatisfaction toward herself and her life. A talented and artistic person, she had come from a well-to-do family and had begun her college career in a respectable manner by joining her mother's sorority and settling down to a major in classics. During her sophomore year she came to the counselor to discuss her newly found "universal religion," which appeared to consist of the belief that "everything that is, is right." Then Janice suddenly announced that she was about to resign her position on the student council and go out on a "big drunk." The counselor was told that this young woman, suffering from an accumulation of tensions within her personality, which took the form of a great desire to burst the bonds of her traditional living, had gone to a faculty member for counsel and had been advised to find some suitable man with whom to have periodic sexual relations. Janice did get drunk, was promptly dismissed from her sorority and escaped expulsion from college only through the efforts of an understanding dean.

The counselor in this case was in a difficult position. If she had become frightened and implored Janice to control and repress her rebellious impulses, she would have found herself cut off immediately from the opportunity to help. Fortunately she was intelligent and courageous, and even though she was unable to save the girl from the minor ''detour'' of getting drunk, she did retain an influence in the situation. Janice did not carry out the sex suggestion—which was fortunate, as mere sexual expression, entered into for its own sake in casual and random fashion, cannot help anyone solve a personality problem, and may make matters worse.

After her spree, Janice attained equilibrium. She shifted her course from classics to sociology and devoted herself to a worthwhile and satisfying college life. She is now doing graduate work in sociology and appears to be on the road to a constructive and useful maturity.

What was the significance of this ''fling'' in Janice's life? Let us notice, first, that it was connected with a change to a *life-affirming religion*. It did represent her naive attempt to affirm the universe. Her change from classics, a relatively formal subject, to sociology represents the same movement toward the affirming of real life. The getting drunk was a grasp at reality, whether successful or not, on the sensuous level. This fling, then, appears to represent Janice's birth throes in her development from formalization to vitality. She was declaring her right to live; this was her war of independence by which she sought the right to fly the flag of her own individual autonomy, all of which unavoidably involved an element of rebellion.

The tendency of most counselors might be to repress such a fling in their counselees, as they well recognize the danger involved. But clearly Janice had this fling in her system, so to speak; and it had to come out in some form if she was ever to become an autonomous individual. The counselor's function, then, was not to forbid the expression, but as much as possible *to direct it into creative channels*.

It not infrequently happens that students, surfeited with subjective academic pursuits, find it necessary to rebel against something. Counselors cannot tell them not to fight, but they can help them to clarify the question of *what* to fight. And there are plenty of evils the fighting of which will furnish William James's "moral equivalent" of getting drunk. Probably it is true that all youths arrive at a stage in their life when they must rebel, have their fling, declare themselves autonomous even though it costs them and others pain. We should not be too frightened at this. It is the sign of vitality, power, potentiality; it is proof of the creative flow of instinctual urges. If adults persuade repression, they may do more harm than good. But counselors can suggest other channels of expression. Youth must sow its oats, but they need not be *wild* oats. So let them sow, but let the oats in their bags be used as constructively as possible. And here is where the courageous counselor can help.

3
Constructive Urges

We have been speaking of the instinctual urges which surge up within every individual, and we have stated that the content of living—including *moral* living—is furnished by the expression of these urges. The person who has attained this healthy self-expression exhibits certain characteristics which we can describe.

Spontaneity is the most obvious characteristic of the person who has learned self-expression. Spontaneity is prized as a virtue because it indicates that the individual has integrated the deeper levels of personality. One has achieved some unity between unconscious urges and conscious aims, and therefore one does not need always to "think twice before one speaks." We have come to terms with our instinctual life, and so we are relieved of the necessity of always being on guard for fear we will do something or say something we will later regret. The spontaneous person acts with more of the whole self. The mere fact that one can do this proves that one has attained some degree of personality health. On the other hand, the individual who has not come to terms with his or her instinctual life, who is always at sharp war with himself or herself, cannot afford to be spontaneous for fear some wild dog will leap out of the unconscious depths and ruin his or her reputation on the spot. We may rightly suspect, therefore, that those who are always carefully controlling themselves in speech and action actually do have particularly antisocial tendencies which they have to keep covered up.

Integrity is another characteristic of the person who has learned healthy self-expression. Integrity means speaking and living from the depths of one's personality; people call this showing one's "real self" to the world, which actually means, again, showing more of one's whole self. We all resent other people being ungenuine in our presence, as we have the impression that their actions and words do not tap any deep level of their being. We have the impression that if such a person were under hypnosis, his or her unconscious mumblings would be quite the opposite of the conscious compliments he or she is paying us, or that upon going home and letting down the artificial props, he or she will proceed to tell his or her spouse what scoundrels we are. Spontaneity and genuineness, when all is said and done, are only forms of elementary honesty. Speaking, acting, living from the depths of one's whole self—this is the ideal.

Another important characteristic of the self-expressive person is *originality*. It goes without saying, but is often forgotten, that every individual is unique, different from every self that has been, is, or will be in the world. When one achieves one's own unique selfhood, one becomes autonomous, an original self directed from within. Our reactions have a certain newness; we move through life like a fresh breeze. We have escaped the life-thwarting straitjacket of the systems of external rules, and tend to become more and more dynamic. We cannot expect to be measured, or to measure others, by the artificial, standardized yardstick of consistency. Nothing is consistent in life—every situation is different from every other, and every person is different today from what he or she was yesterday. Thus one who has achieved one's originality is able better to meet the ever-changing crises of life. One has become part of the infinite creativity of the life process and it is expressed in the unique creativity of one's own self. One's living surges up from within; this it is that gives strength and convincingness to personality.

It follows that new forms of *freedom* are a special characteristic of the individual who has come to terms with instinctual urges. One cannot be free while one's consciousness is locked in warfare with pressures from unconsciousness. That is why the aim of psychotherapeutic treatment is often summed up as "setting the individual free"—free from special inhibitions and repressions, from childhood fixations, from training formulas, and so on. One feels pity for the great majority of people that they should be enslaved by unnecessary fears. One sees them going through life carrying psychological burdens which keep them from freedom even more in actuality than the prisoner's iron ball and chain. It is a truism that most people develop to only a third or less of their personality possibilities. The counselor will aim to set people free so that they can develop into their unique, autonomous selves and realize some of the untapped potentialities in personality.

To live the life of self-expression requires courage. To love greatly, to admit one's hate without having it destroy one's equilibrium, to express anger when it is genuine, to rise to heights of joy and to know deep sorrow, to go on far adventures in spite of loneliness, to catch lofty ideas and carry them into action—in short, to live out the infinite number of instinctual urges that rise in glorious challenge within one requires courage. We must not hold back out of cowardice. We must have the "courage of imperfection," as Adler often said, to overcome petty inhibitions, to move ahead in spite of all our little worries, to triumph over the burden of unnecessary fears. People are inclined to hold back because they know the way ahead is lined with dangers. But this holding back is often the beginning of their personality problems—the stream of life will not be dammed. The counselor seeks to give people courage to live, to help them overcome the unnecessary fears, the dread of meeting people, the fear of falling in love, the anxieties that may seize them on taking a new job. What a great proportion of the anxieties that attack people are

unnecessary and useless! There is reason for the deep anxiety inherent in the tragic possibilities of living, as will be discussed
below; but the infinite number of little fears and worries each
day simply hold people back from creative living. Human beings
cannot stand still; they must move on or they stagnate, knowing
that there are great possibilities for evil ahead as well as for good.

Yes, the artesian wells within the individual must not be
stopped up; the stream of life, with all its instinctual impulses
and emotional colors, must flow on. It is the counselor's aim to
give people who come to him or her broken in courage a glimpse
of the possibilities ahead for joy and achievement. From this point
of view, the great prophets of the life of self-expression are right:
Rousseau when he cries, "Ah! to live must be a beautiful thing!"[2]
and calls on people to live themselves out to the full. And Nietzsche, when he rightly charges that " 'virtue,' in my opinion, has
been *more* injured by the *tediousness* of its advocates than by
anything else,"[3] and challenges people to be "free spirits," to
express themselves heroically, as "supermen."

X   *Religion and Mental Health*

Harold was a young minister, newly graduated from the seminary and in the process of settling down in his first parish. He was planning to be married within a few months, but he was afraid the marriage would have to be postponed because of his poor health. He feared a complete nervous breakdown. In fact, he was already on the verge of it; he was so nervous that it was difficult for him to continue his work, and his friends had advised him to give up the parish and take a complete rest for a few months.

Harold said his nervousness came from his continual worrying. He could not stop worrying—that was the problem he brought to the counselor. He had tried to "beat down" this worrying, to use his own very descriptive term, but his efforts had been in vain. An inferiority "complex" had troubled him for a number of years. He felt inferior, he said, to everyone with whom he talked.

As counselor I noticed that his body was thin, his complexion sallow, his eyes faded and flighty, and I observed that he did not sit still but fidgeted about continually. Another sign of nervousness was his habit of changing the subject abruptly. He spoke of the woman whom he was about to marry as a good church organist and a Sunday school teacher of long experience. The chief motive in his choice of her appeared to be her suitability as a minister's wife and a helper in the church work.

He could not understand why he should be in poor health as he had given up smoking while in college, then coffee and tea, and in an entirely serious voice he said he had just recently added cocoa to the list of his renunciations. He had renounced smoking and drinking because of his ideal of keeping his body the "temple of God." During college he had also given up card playing, dancing, and swearing in order not "to lower his ideals and go the way of the other fellows who did these things." He had always been particularly discriminating about people with whom he associated, and in his present parish he was careful not to be seen on the street with women who were not "respectable." The young people of the town danced and played cards, and when they asked him why he did not, he answered that dancing was a sin for him, but, "I can't say what it is for you; you may be strong enough to do it."

What is wrong with Harold?

1
Neurotic Religion

He is already in the process of a nervous breakdown. If he had not told us that, we could have assumed it, as the style of life he described would lead inevitably to such a personality crisis.

He was right in stressing his inferiority feeling; we observe that his style of life is constructed around a basic feeling of insecurity so exhaustively that he must strive morally and religiously to compensate, and those efforts failing, he would finally take refuge in a nervous breakdown. His renunciations, we may assume, are for the purpose of raising his own moral prestige above that of the persons around him. He has told us in so many words that this was his technique in making himself superior to his college fellows. And it is now his way of triumphing over the other persons in his town. This basic feeling of insecurity is evidenced in his great desire to be "respectable"; inwardly he feels that he is not. He is even using his marriage as a rung on this ladder of egocentricity by which he climbs to moral and religious triumph. If his fiancee's ability to fit in as a minister's wife is his chief motive in marrying her, as we have reason to assume, he is actually marrying her for what she can do to further his own success. Such a motive can lead only to failure in the marriage.

Some persons, observing how he was using religion to bolster his egocentric style of life, would advise Harold to throw religion out of his life altogether. As a matter of fact, this might do some good. In getting rid of his false religion, Harold would be forced ultimately to find some elements of authentic religion. The counselor, however, would proceed not by this crude method but by helping him to understand his basic feeling of inferiority which drives him to his senseless moral and religious competition. It can be hoped that this would help him develop an inner security and genuine courage.

Using Harold's case as a basis, let us pick out some tests by which to discover and guard against the neurotic tendencies in religious living. We observe, first, that Harold's religion served as a barrier between him and other people; indeed its *raison d'etre* was the forming of this barrier. Great religious teachers, though they have often been forced to break with the superficial demands of their society, have emphasized their especially deep attachment to others. We may conclude that religion has a dangerous neurotic tendency whenever it separates one from other human beings.

We observe, in the second place, that Harold's religion did not appeal to his courage but to his weakness. It was the instrument by which his ego attempted to attain a false security. There is nothing to be disparaged in religion's allaying the feeling of insecurity; indeed, to give the individual *true* security is one of the basic functions of religion. But the dangerous tendency is that religious individuals, like Harold, endeavor to gain that security by shortcuts which lead only into the woods of illusion and never arrive back on the road of true security. Thus, being an instrument primarily for meeting weakness, these strategies ensconced him further into his state of dependence and immaturity. He is a clear demonstration of Nietzsche's charge that Christianity, as practiced in his day, was an expression of cowardice. It can be concluded that religion, of whatever type, tends to become neurotic whenever *it appeals to one's weakness more than to one's strength*.

And finally, in the case of Harold, where was the "life abundant"? His life was cramped, cold, frightened. What joy he got was in his egoistic triumph over others; he was already in the first stages of a breakdown, nature's stamp of disapproval upon a way of life. Where is the sense of adventure and the simple, calm joys based on trust in life? Whether Christian or Buddhism or Sufism or some other religion, the practice becomes neurotic whenever *it cramps and impoverishes life, thus destroying the possibility of living abundantly*.

Observing how neurotic individuals often take to religion, Freud concluded that religion itself abets neurosis. Religion is a means, he stated, by which the human being ensconces himself or herself in a childlike state of dependence and protection. Being frightened by the deep insecurity of life, shrinking from facing the world with all its disappointments and hardships, human beings set up a religious system by which they can revert to the protection a child enjoys from its father and mother. The dogmas of the religious system which make possible belief in intelligence, purpose, and moral law in the universe "are illusions, fulfillments of the oldest, strongest and most insistent wishes of mankind."[1] Religion appeals to our neurotic tendencies; in fact, "religion would be the universal obsessional neurosis of humanity."[2] Freud concluded by prophesying that with the advancement of the human race and the progress of science, religion will gradually be abandoned.

It must be admitted that there is a great deal of truth in these charges. Some people obviously *do* use religion as a means of buttressing themselves in a halfway state of development, constructing for themselves a nest of false security and protection from which they can view life as a sweet and rosy protection which takes care of all true believers. The longing for the cults is illustrated by thousands of converts to the Moonies, Radjneeshians, etc., despite the fact that many individuals get real, or at least temporary, help from them. The question always is, what happens in the long run? We cannot forget the Rev. Jim Jones and the mass suicide of his 919 followers in Gyana, because Jones ordered them to do so.

As a matter of fact, *all aspects of culture can be used this way when seized upon by neurotic individuals*. Literature can be a flight from life, abetting ill health, but it can also be an efficacious way to promote psychological zest and spiritual meaning. The same is true of philosophy and art, and subjects which Rank calls "the great spontaneous therapies of man."[3]

The *abuse* of religion is what Freud is attacking. And to that extent he is right and has much of crucial value to teach us. But authentic religion, namely a *fundamental affirmation of the meaning of life*, is something quite else. It is the latter we are concerned with here.

2

Passion for Meaning

The neurotic attitude can best be described as an inability to *affirm*. "Affirm" means more than merely "accept"; it is accepting actively, saying "yes" not only verbally or mentally but as

a response of one's total personality. Neurotics cannot affirm relationships; they are at war with the human predicament. As we
have pointed out, they regard other people with basic suspicion
and hostility. They cannot affirm the universe—it, too, is the
enemy, the work of Satan or Mephistophales. "We have been
hurled from mother's womb against our wishes," they seem to
be telling us, "and we long to go back into the womb again."

This lack of ability to affirm one's self, one's fellows and the
universe, is obviously connected with the neurotic's accentuated
feeling of insecurity. Neurotics do not accept the fact that everyone
feels insecure: the anxiety is part of the price we pay for living
as individuals. Religion ideally is an aid to turn neurotic anxiety
into normal, creative anxiety. The neurotics, differing from
healthy persons, cannot come to terms with this insecurity—it
gives them too much anxiety; it paralyzes action and throws personality into panic.

Inability to affirm is merely another term for inability to *trust*.
Not being able to trust, the neurotic lacks *confidence* and the
related quality, *courage*. He or she must, therefore, endeavor to
remain dependent in some situation of false security.

These qualities are linked together. If neurotic people had
the power to trust, and collaterally confidence and courage, they
could give an affirmative answer to life. And giving this affirmative answer, they would in a measure affirm their security and
be fitted then to overcome the anxiety constructively. Because
of the inability to affirm, they are caught in a vicious circle, which
we saw led ultimately to nervous breakdown. The universe, which
actually is neutral so far as values go, is taken by them to be hostile,
and so they construct various compensating pictures of heaven
and an afterlife.

I am not making judgments; I am seeking to describe our
human anxiety and the way we meet it.

This is ultimately a religious problem whether the person concludes it in those terms or not. If one could have confidence in
life's meaning, could believe in the ultimate value of one's self
and others, could have confidence that the universe has meaning in which one's own insecurity can be overcome, then one could

experience the confidence and courage which one needs to live. Jung's oft-quoted statement puts it well:

> "Among all my patients in the second half of life—that is to say, over thirty-five—there has not been one whose problem in the last resort was not that of finding a religious outlook on life. It is safe to say that every one of them fell ill because he had lost that which the living religions of every age have given to their followers, and none of them has been really healed who did not regain his religious outlook."[4]

This holds, broadly speaking, for persons in the first half of life as well. It is the problem of the individual's finding meaning in his or her own life and ultimately meaning in the life process. What one needs to live, says Jung, is "faith, hope, love, and insight."[5]

To approach the question from the negative side, let us ask what happens to mental health when this meaning which religion gives is absent. In other words, what is the effect of atheism on personality?

3
Atheism as Discouragement

Frank was a real atheist. At the time of this interview, he was a sophomore in college, an intellectually brilliant young man from a cultured background. But he was not getting on well. He was studying very little and hence was in academic difficulties in spite of his high intelligence. He was not looking forward to any particular vocation; in fact, he seemed to have no engrossing interests. He spent his time reading widely but superficially, getting drunk, and leading a reckless sort of social life. Indeed, he was continually in such an oppressive state of melancholy that drinking and using women as his playthings were his only means of relief. He was, of course, cynical; he rarely smiled when he talked to me, and in general he was very unhappy. His home background had been neutral with the respect to religion, and he claimed himself an atheist.

Most persons who call themselves atheists actually are not, but there is no doubt that Frank was. The proof of the matter is that there was no meaning of any sort, practically speaking, in his life. His personality was disintegrating; he was, as we should expect, bristling with problems. He felt no purpose in his living. And from a psychological point of view, he was clearly neurotic.

I have been startled by the fact that practically every genuine atheist with whom I have dealt has exhibited unmistakable neurotic tendencies.* How can we account for this curious fact? Is it merely that we tend to classify atheists as neurotics because they are, by definition, in rebellion against one aspect of accepted culture? Yes, to some extent.

But there is a deeper reason. We observe that the distinguishing characteristic of Frank was his lack of purpose. Of course, his personality was disintegrating as there was no core. It was more than a question of maladjustment of tensions—there was a lack of pattern around which any adjustment could be made. This is why a denial of purpose, either in his or her own life or in life as a whole, is so serious for the neurotic. He or she has no style of life, for his life is not moving in any direction. Consequently, Frank could find no meaning in his existence. Life was to him indeed a "tale, Told by an idiot, full of sound and fury, Signifying nothing." This is a state of neurosis which can be described by the religious term "hell"; the gradual disintegration, the breakdown in unity, the fighting of one's self and everything else are certainly a hell if ever such existed.

Every individual needs some belief in purpose, however fragmentary, to achieve any kind of personality health. Without

*I do not at all mean persons like John Dewey or, for that matter, Freud himself. They obviously have much meaning in their lives. I define atheism as the "theoretical formulation of the discouraged life."

purpose there is no meaning; and without meaning one, in the end, cannot live. Purpose serves in personality like a steel core in an electromagnet—it unifies the lines of force into a pattern, and thus enables the magnet to exert effective power.

Personality health also requires that the individual believe in some purpose in the total life process as well as in his or her own life. One cannot live on an island of meaning surrounded by an ocean of meaninglessness. If the universe is crazy, the parts of it must be crazy too. This supports the original statement above, that neurotics need to affirm themselves and society and the universe; the three aspects of affirmation of life go together.

This is what constitutes religion. Religion is the belief in the total life process. Not, of course, the religion of a Harold or of any dogmatic sect, but religion as a basic attitude with which we confront our existence.

Jung finds the needed meaning in the deepest levels of the collective unconscious. Here is the source of the idea of God, an archetype, a ''primordial image.''

> ''The idea of an all-powerful divine being is present everywhere, if not consciously recognized, then unconsciously accepted, because it is an archetype. . . . Therefore I consider it wiser to recognize the idea of God consciously; otherwise something else becomes God, as a rule something quite inappropriate and stupid.''[6]

In the healing process of the neurotic, says Jung, ''the archetypes come to independent life and serve as spiritual guides for the personality, thus supplanting the inadequate ego with its futile willing and striving. As a religious-minded person would say: guidance has come from God . . . I must express myself in more modest terms and say that the psyche has awakened to spontaneous life.''[7] Finding religion consists of discovering these deep levels of the unconscious and assimilating them into one's conscious living. Jung describes people who achieve thus:

> ''They came to themselves, they could accept themselves, they were able to become reconciled to themselves, and by this they

were also reconciled to adverse circumstances and events. This is much like what was formerly expressed by saying: He has made his peace with God, he has sacrificed his own will, he has submitted himself to the will of God."[8]

Defining God as an archetype sounds strange to modern ears, but it has good theological support in history. It is similar to Plato's Idea of the Good, the ultimate idea or archetype which he calls God. Christian mystics have often talked of finding God in the deepest stratum of the self, the collective unconscious, where subjectivity and objectivity are overcome, "In the depths of the soul," said Augustine, "thought and being are one."

Jung's explanation of religious experience is stimulating and helpful, but it is incomplete. It emphasizes God's immanence in the individual, but its danger is in stopping here and identifying God with the deep levels in one's self. In other words, is God only your unconscious self, or what is not very different from a qualitative point of view, the collective selves of a group of people? Jung's view requires balance by an emphasis on the transcendent nature of God, which we find in the historical struggles shown in theology.

4
Counseling and the Infinite

The deeper one's thought penetrates in the field of psychotherapy, the closer one comes to the realm of theology. Psychotherapy begins with the problem of how the neurotic individual is to live most effectively; this becomes the finding of meaning in the neurotic's life, and at this point psychotherapy finds itself dealing with theology. The fundamental questions with which psychotherapy ends point toward the field of theology.

We found this true in our original analysis of personality in the first two chapters. There it was discovered that any adequate picture of personality must take into consideration the tension in human nature between what is and what ought to be. This is stated theologically as the contradiction between sin in human nature on the one hand and response to the universal structure, or God, on the other. It will be remembered that the psychotherapists Jung and Rank frankly recognized this contradiction, which they termed the "dualism" in human nature, and explicitly admitted their dependence on theology for answers to this universal quest.

Human beings would indeed find themselves in an impossible situation, which seems to be back again with the song "Amazing Grace." Grace is a theological term but it has its corresponding term in psychotherapy, "clarification." When neurotic individuals are caught in the vicious circle of egocentricity, and they cannot adequately bear the tension which freedom lays upon them and so misuse their autonomy in self-defeating egocentricity, they are enabled by clarification to break the throttling clutch of egocentricity.

We can learn much from the practices of Alcoholics Anonymous, the one method which has had success in helping alcoholics and drug addicts to control their habit. The essential aspect of treatment at the beginning is the alcoholic's *despair*. The addict's belief that he or she can stop drinking by choice is mercilessly attacked; only by giving up completely will the addict find relief. If the new member does not experience despair, the other members take pains to attack his or her "false ego" until he or she admits despair.

The other essential prerequisite for overcoming addiction is the belief in some force in the universe greater than one's self, whatever form this belief may take. This enables the addict to believe in a curative power beyond the self, a power which is not egocentric.

What happens psychologically we can describe as follows: The neurotic individual has finally suffered so much that he or she is willing to renounce anything, even life if need be. The person is in that state in which he or she is able to say, "Not my will but thine be done," and at that moment feels he or she is not significant as a self-willing creature, but significant only because he or she can be to some small extent the channel of meaning of the universe. Fortunately, the structure of the universe has been there all the time with its call; and upon becoming able to respond, the individual is able to act without a predominantly egocentric motive. Because one has lost one's life, one has found it.

One is right in calling this the *grace of God*, as it is preposterous to think that the individual does it for himself or herself. People give up, and the healing force of the universe, if one wishes to term it that, comes to their rescue. It is not that they deserve it; only when they get over thinking they deserve it are they in a position to receive help.

There is a sense of putting oneself on the line, the sense of *wager* which famous men have described. The psychologist and philosopher William James was subjected to deep depressions in his late twenties, so he tells us in his autobiography, while studying psychology in Europe. He could not believe in human freedom. The conviction seemed to overpower him that his actions were all *re*actions, like Pavlov's dogs; his own aims had nothing to do with the results. James was in such a depression over many months that he seriously considered suicide.

Finally it occurred to him that he could *bet* on freedom, that he could resolve at the beginning of each day that he would believe in freedom for that day. He found his wager worked. His belief in freedom turned out to *be* his freedom.

Another example is Blaise Pascal, the seventeenth century French physicist. Pascal called his discovery by the same name; he made a *wager* that there is meaning in the universe. If he was right in positing God, as he described it, he would be happier and life would have meaning; and if he was wrong, he would lose nothing. This sense of wagering one's life, we can add, is as valid psychologically as it is religiously. One needs to take a chance, to posit one's life, and then the conclusion has a dynamic, a power, that it did not have before.

Thus one experiences a "cosmic humility," which relieves us of our burden of arrogance; we avoid *hubris*, as the classical Greeks would say. We sense more than previously our own worth in the respect that as a personality we participate in the divine logos of meaning and we can understand flashes of it now and then. We take the attitude of "giving back" to the universe some of the debt we as creatures owe—and this is the root of the valid feeling of *duty*. We will recognize that there are purposes which swing in arcs greater than our own, and we will aim to put ourselves in harmony with them.

This clarification, or experience of grace if you will, does not happen once and for all, so that thereafter the individual can proceed with never a care. Those who think they have been "saved" and thus relieved permanently from the fundamental tension of life have missed the point. They have fallen into a "slough of despond," the false "sanctification" which is even more subtly egocentric.

This experience is a new ordering of tensions in personality, and an adjustment that must continually be remade. There is a peak experience, as Maslow put it, a "conversion" after the climax of suffering and the sudden influx of understanding. But the grace must be a continuous gift, just as clarification is. It is important for the clarified individuals to remember that they still have the "old Adam" within their consciousness, but they are able to confront this egocentric tendency creatively. We are not suddenly carried off into a blissful state. The tension remains, but clarification (here we use the term as synonymous with grace) has removed the poison from the fangs of egocentricity. People still tend to make selfish decisions; but through their awareness of the tendency, their living is much less egocentric in motivation.

This "giving up" does not at all mean that we renounce our creativity, thereby tending to become static and unproductive. On the contrary, the achievement of grace and clarification of which we speak effects precisely the most creative adjustment of tensions within us. Our egocentricity has been the block to our creativity. Freed to an extent at least from that, we are able to express creativity directly, spontaneously, and gratifyingly. In the words of St. Paul, the fetters of the law have been removed, and the spirit is able to rise up on its own wings. There is a creativity of grace. In this the individual does not waste energies struggling against inhibitions and constrictions. But the freed energies of the artist, no longer absorbed in wrestling with the self, can woo beauty with an experience of freedom.

Clarification and grace do not wipe the guilt away, but one is enabled to accept and affirm the guilt. The very accepting of it, the realization of it—which is classically termed "repentance"—is connected with the coming of grace. The fact that guilt, or sin, or egocentricity, or whatever one may term it, is never completely wiped away proves the importance of humility in the experience. There is no, "Lord, I thank thee that I am not as other men." Presumptuous satisfaction in one's own salvation is out of place both religiously and psychologically. This is so because the more clarified one becomes, the more one realizes one's imperfect human condition. The paradox is understandable that those who are most sensitive to universal grace should call themselves the "chief of sinners," as the saints through history have taught.

Some people accept and affirm only what is good in themselves, and affirm the universe only so long as it is good to them. This is an error into which our utopian tendencies lead us, and it misses the deeper aspects of life. It is as though one would affirm only a blissful world, about which one could sing, "God's in his heaven, all's right with the world." If all were right with the world, there would be no meaning in personality, and certainly no need for counselors or therapists.

In the human situation, all is not right; there is disharmony within the self, and there is disharmony in this diseased world. Psychologically and religiously, illness follows from any attempt to escape this disharmony. It is the pampered child, Adler would say, who is willing to play only so long as the universe plays his or her way.

The healthy individual, on the other hand, is willing to walk the knife-blade edge of insecurity and to affirm truth and goodness even though truth is on the scaffold and goodness is never perfectly achieved. Job teaches us much here, namely, the necessity of affirming goodness even though the individual experiences little of it. The reward of mental and religious health comes to us when we are able to cry with Job, ''Though He slay me, yet will I trust Him.'' A unique sense of freedom comes over one after the experience of clarification and grace. Such individuals have at last found themselves, and found their fellow human beings as well as their place in the universe.

REFERENCES AND NOTES

CHAPTER I

1. A very brief *historical sketch* of the development of psychotherapy may be apropos here. This includes several of the great historical philosophers who made special contributions to our understanding of personality.

   Its roots are to be seen far back in Socrates' philosophy, illustrated in such maxims as, "Know thyself," and, "Knowledge is virtue," which reappear particularly in modern Adlerian thought. Plato exhibits profound insights on love and the nature of the unconscious which have their modern counterparts, especially in Jungianism. Ancient Stoicism made great endeavors to subject psychological processes to rational control; *vide* Marcus Aurelius' *Meditations*. We do not have space to indicate the importance of such early philosophies as Epicureanism, or early Christian mysticism. But Augustine should be mentioned as one of the most profound of early psychologists; his idea that in the depths of the individual soul the cleavage between subjectivity and objectivity is overcome is a classic statement still valid as the central presupposition of psychotherapy.

   Descartes (seventeenth century) set the problem which psychotherapy aims to solve in his unfortunate separation of mind from bodily functions. Then Spinoza endeavored to set up a scheme of psychological control of one's self by very rationalistic means. His ideas that the quality of our happiness depends on the things we love, that the things we fear are harmful only in our minds, that every passion is a confused idea and can be clarified by calm understanding, show a psychological understanding which is penetrating even if incomplete (see his *Ethics*).

   Rousseau (eighteenth century) is exceedingly important as one of the chief figures in the romantic movement upon which modern psychotherapy depends. In his living, thinking, and preaching, Rousseau embodied the emotionalism, the rebellion against the restraints of society, and the "back to nature" cravings which romantics have always felt, and which take a prominent place in modern psychotherapeutic thought (*cf.* Freud's *Civilization and Its Discontents*). These aspects of Rousseau's thought are basic in later psychotherapy: vitalism (or emphasis on life force), reaction against rationalism, individualism, confidence in nature. He believed in self-expression, living one's self out to the full. His definition of education as a "direct and unconscious unfolding of the individual" (*Emile*) has surprising affinities with the Adlerian view. His confidence in the goodness of human nature also comes out in Adlerian thought.

Schopenhauer and Nietzsche (nineteenth century) are important precursors of psychotherapy, the former in his development of the "will and idea" problem, and the latter in his amazingly astute psychological insights. Nietzsche was a psychoanalyst who in many ways predicted later trends. He sensed something of the meaning of dreams. His introspection disclosed to him many truths regarding the function of the unconscious; he realized that the conclusions of the philosophers were actually pictures of their own deep selves, and that external problems were only stepping stones to the central area, namely self-knowledge. He saw that inner conflicts can be "sublimated" into art or striving for power. His idea that "instinct is the most intelligent of all kinds of intelligence" (*Beyond Good and Evil*, p. 162) has curiously close parallels in statements of Jung. His concept of "will to power" has resemblance to Adler's central idea of the universal striving for power, but in reality Nietzsche is more Freudian. The negative view of society, the excessive laudation of individual strength, and the idea that all moral categories should be transcended in the end, are concepts which Nietzsche and Freud hold in common. They both see that instinctual expression leads in the end to destruction; but Nietzsche makes of this a tragic life-view, whereas Freud ends in pessimism.

The development of science in the nineteenth century also had an important influence on psychotherapy. Here Freud obtained his devotion to the scientific method and his belief that it is possible to bring human emotions and mind under control by analysis just as science brings the natural order under its control.

In the development of modern psychotherapy itself, Sigmund Freud, in his work beginning the last of the nineteenth century, is unchallengably the pioneer. Jung and Adler, originally associated with Freud, broke from him to establish their own schools in the early years of this century. Jung terms his branch "Analytic Psychology," and Adler his "Individual Psychology," to distinguish them from Freud's "Psychoanalysis." Rank deviated from the Freudian school only a few years ago. Fritz Kunkel began as an Adlerian and developed certain unique contributions of his own.

Thus, in the roots of modern psychotherapy, we find the thought streams of *romanticism, rationalism*, and *science* all important. In general psychotherapy can be designated as romantic in its metaphysical presuppositions, rationalistic in many of its practices (particularly Adlerianism), and scientific in its general technique (especially Freudianism).

2. Freud has written a great number of works dealing with various aspects of his system, and there are available innumerable semi-authoritative expositions by members of the Freudian school. To recommend a single book, however, we should cite as the most useful the recent *New Introductory Lectures on Psychoanalysis*, which presents the central Freudian theses in their more profound and developed form.

3. *A General Introduction to Psychoanalysis*, p. 375.

4. "There is nothing undetermined in the psychic life." *The Psychopathology of Everyday Life*, p. 282.

5. "Psychoanalysis extends the region of science to the mind of mankind." *New Introductory Lectures on Psychoanalysis*, p. 218. In this section Freud holds that science is the only admissible form of human knowledge, and in the final chapter of this book he explains his devotion to science as the hope of mankind. Freud's overvaluation of the scientific method and human reason are to be seen in such statements as, "It would be an illusion to suppose that we could get anywhere else what it (science) cannot give us" (*Future of an Illusion*, p. 98), and, "There is no appeal beyond reason" (*ibid*., p. 49). For a discussion of the true function of science, and an explanation of the general failure to recognize the limits of science, of which Freudianism is an example, see Whitehead's *The Function of Reason*.

Rank's criticism is to the point: "The psychoanalytic striving to educate the individual exclusively in natural science, casual thinking, which Freud advocates in his last writing (*Der Zukunft einer Illusion*, 1927) is fortunately not possible, but betrays his whole moralistic pedagogical attitude, the very opposite of the attitude necessary for a constructive therapy of the individual." *Will Therapy*, p. 62.

6. I am indebted to Professor Paul Tillich for this viewpoint.

7. Otto Rank's recent books, *Will Therapy* and *Truth and Reality*, give stimulating and profound discussions of the function of will

in personality and the importance of such qualities as freedom, personal autonomy, and moral responsibility.

8. The central importance of creative will in Rank's view of personality is indicated in such statements as, "the creative type is able to create voluntarily from the impulsive elements and moreover to develop his standards beyond identifications of the super-ego morality to an ideal formation which consciously guides and rules this creative will in terms of personality. The essential point in this process is the fact that he evolves his ego ideal from himself, not merely on the ground of given but also of self-chosen factors which he strives after consciously." *Truth and Reality*, p. 9.

   Rank explains that this conception of creative, personal autonomy "makes creative power and creative accomplishment comprehensible for the first time, rather than the insipid and impotent concept of sublimation, which prolongs a shadowy existence in psychoanalysis." *Ibid.*, p. 11.

9. Another aspect of Rank's thought is especially significant for us, namely, his idea that the neurotic is the "artiste manque," the artist, that is, who cannot produce any art. The neurotic is the individual who desires to create—in fact, is forced to create, which in the long last is all anyone is forced to do in life—but for some reason cannot produce any creative work. Thus the neurotic, or for that matter any individual with a pronounced personality difficulty, may well be precisely the individual who possesses unusual creative potentialities, but is unable to adjust the tensions within his personality so as to bring these powers into effective expression. "I attempt to show in the neurotic," says Rank, "the superhuman, divine spark." *Will Therapy*, p. 141.

10. *Truth and Reality*, p. 66.

11. "If a man so thinks, feels, and acts, in a word so lives, as to correspond directly with objective conditions and their claims, whether in a good sense or ill, he is extroverted." *Psychological Types*, p. 417.

12. *Modern Man in Search of a Soul*, p. 69.

13. *Ibid.*, p. 69. Jung's broad emphasis upon the force and influence of unconscious and irrational factors in living is illustrated in such statements as, "The unconscious is capable at times of assuming an intelligence and purposiveness which are superior to actual conscious insight" (*Psychology and Religion*, p. 45), and, "In human affairs what appears impossible upon the way of the intellect has very often become true upon the way of the irrational. Indeed, all the greatest changes that have ever affected mankind have come

not by the way of intellectual calculation, but by ways which con-temporary minds either ignored or rejected as absurd, and which only long afterwards became fully recognized through their intrin-sic necessity" (*Psychological Types*, p. 113). Consequently Jung places great value upon fantasy: "But what great thing ever came into existence that was not first phantasy?" (*Ibid.*, p. 77.) "It is not the artist alone, but every creative individual whatsoever who owes all that is greatest in his life to phantasy. The dynamic prin-ciple of phantasy is 'play,' which belongs also to the child, and as such it appears to be inconsistent with the principle of serious work. But without this playing with phantasy no creative work has ever yet come to birth." (*Ibid.*, p. 82.)

14. *Modern Man in Search of a Soul*, p. 190.
15. Jung states that his "archetypes" are identical with the Platonic "ideas." The archetypes, he says, are like "ideas born in one's blood." (Quoted from a lecture.)
16. "Artistic disposition involves an overweight of collective psychic life as against the personal. Art is a kind of innate drive that seizes a human being and makes him its instrument. . . . The artist . . . is 'man' in a higher sense—he is 'collective man'—one who car-ries and shapes the unconscious, psychic life of mankind." (*Modern Man in Search of a Soul*, p. 195.) "Whenever the creative force predominates, human life is ruled and moulded by the unconscious as against the active will, and the conscious ego is swept along on a subterranean current, being nothing more than a helpless observer of events." (*Ibid.*, p. 197.) "The secret of artistic creation and of the effectiveness of art is to be found in a return to the state of *participation mystique*—to that level of experience at which it is man who lives, and not the individual, and at which the weal or woe of the single human being does not count, but only human existence." (*Ibid.*, p. 198, 199.)

CHAPTER II

1. It may be interesting to pass on some impressions of Dr. Adler the man, with whom I have had the prized privilege of studying, associating, and conversing intimately. Dr. Adler was the kind of person the French term "sympatique"; to talk with him was to have that rare privilege of a human relationship without barriers. One of his chief characteristics was his ability to remain relaxed, even in discussion; it was impossible to feel tense in his company. The

criticism of superficiality that is leveled against some of his ideas is to an extent justified, but it is none the less true that his system as a whole will go down in history as a lasting contribution to the endeavor of man to understand himself.

2. Adler describes the ego as having much more power as a directing agent than the Freudian ego.

   One of the chief differences between the Adlerian and Freudian systems is in the respect that Adler emphasizes the present *purpose* of the individual rather than the determining factors in his background. His system is teleological rather than causological. Whereas Freud deals chiefly with the causative factors in the individual's past, such as childhood experiences, Adler concerns himself with the direction in which the individual is moving.

3. Probably the most useful single book of Adler's is the readable *Understanding Human Nature*.

4. *What Life Should Mean to You*.

5. Jung is very outspoken on this point: "But individuation means precisely a better and more complete fulfilment of the collective dispositions of mankind, since an adequate consideration of the peculiarity of the individual is more conducive to a better social achievement, than when the peculiarity is neglected or repressed." (*Two Essays in Analytical Psychology*, p. 184.)

6. Freud says in one place that guilt feeling is an expression of the tension between the ego and the super-ego (*New Introductory Lectures on Psychoanalysis*, p. 88), and in another that it represents a masochistic tendency toward self punishment. But Freud does not understand the nature of the normal guilt feeling of which we are speaking, as he does not understand the role of freedom, autonomy, and responsibility in personality. His naturalism confines him to the existential level; and hence no genuine guilt feeling, such as leads to religious tension, is admissible. As Rank says, "In Psychoanalytic theory . . . *guilt feeling is and remains a final insoluble fact* (*Truth and Reality*, p. 32).

7. This is what Thomas Mann has in mind when he quotes Degas as saying, "A picture must be painted with the same feeling as that with which a criminal commits his crime." Then Mann adds, "This is the precious and guilty secret," as he refers to Goethe's refusal to talk about his creative projects when he was in the process of producing them. (*Freud, Goethe and Wagner*, p. 85.)

8. *Truth and Reality*, p. 62. The quotation continues, ". . . and even if there were none of the numerous proofs for the inner freedom of conscious will, the fact of human consciousness of guilt alone

would be sufficient to prove the freedom of the will as we understand it psychologically beyond a doubt." And, "In a word, will
and guilt are the two complementary sides of one and the same
phenomenon." (*Ibid.*, p. 62.)

9. This has been spoken of historically as the "dualism" in man's
nature. To indicate that we are still on good psychological ground,
let us quote Rank and Jung on the matter. "Man suffers from a
fundamental dualism, however one may formulate it, and not from
a conflict created by forces in the environment which might be
avoided by a 'correct bringing up' or removed by later re-education
(psychoanalysis." (*Will Therapy*, p. 173.) Jung speaks of it in the
terms of St. Paul, "old Adam" and the "new man." Each extreme
is "salvaging only a narrow state of consciousness. The alternative
is to shatter it with the tension inherent in the play of opposites—
in the dualistic stage—and thereby to build up a state of wider and
higher consciousness." (*Modern Man in Search of a Soul*, p. 117.)
Putting on the "new man" does not mean getting rid of the "old
Adam." Being aware of one's divided state is the third and highest
step in consciousness.

CHAPTER IV

1. *Psychological Types*, p. 368. Also, "But since the feeling-into subject feels his activity, his life, into the object, he therewith also yields
himself to the object."

2. *Understanding Human Nature*, pp. 60 , 61.

3. *Modern Man in Search of a Soul*, p. 57. Jung also says here: "We
cannot by any device bring it about that the treatment is not the
outcome of a mutual influence in which the whole being of the
patient as well as that of the doctor plays its part. Two primary
factors come together in the treatment—that is, two persons, neither
of whom is a fixed and determinable magnitude. . . . You can
exert no influence if you are not susceptible to influence. It is futile
for the doctor to shield himself from the influence of the patient
and to surround himself with a smoke-screen of fatherly and professional authority." (This whole book is to be recommended to
every counselor.)

4. *How Natives Think*, p. 364. Other quotations from this important book pertain to our point: "Every individual *is* both such and
such a man or woman, alive at present, a certain ancestral individual, who may be human or semi-human . . . and at the same

time he *is* his totem, that is, he partakes in mystic fashion of the essence of the animal or vegetable species whose name he bears. . . . The verb 'to be' . . . encompasses both the collective representation and the collective consciousness in a participation that is actually lived, in a kind of symbiosis effected by identity of essence.'' (*Ibid.*, p. 91.)

"Now the need of participation assuredly remains something more imperious and more intense, even among peoples like ourselves, than the thirst for knowledge and the desire for conformity with the claims of reason. It lies deeper within us and its source is more remote.'' (*Ibid.*, p. 385.)

5. *Ibid.*, p. 385.
6. It is not sentimentality, then, to speak of the power of faith to bring about a change in another individual. Faith in a person, be it the mother's in her child, or the young man's in his friend, or the wife's in her husband, actually does create a strong force for the strengthening or transforming of the other personality. This is an old religious truth which here receives psychological confirmation on the basis of our understanding of empathy.
7. *New Introductory Lectures*, pp. 78 ff. Freud believes that the balance of evidence at the moment is in favor of mental telepathy, and requests a more favorable attitude toward it. But he attempts, to my mind mistakenly, to interpret telepathy as a more complicated and subtle form of physical transference, like the telephone. There is no more reason for hypothesizing telepathy as sensory than as *extra*-sensory.
8. *Psychopathology of Everyday Life*, p. 255. Freud's explanation of his honesty follows: "As often as I attempt a distortion I succumb to an error or some other faulty act, which betrays my dishonesty.'' This proves our point, namely, that the psychologically rectified mind becomes more honest by dint of its own automatic processes.
9. Freud's explanation of the phenomenon of influence hinges on his theory of the superego, the parental function in the mind which sits in judgment, as it were, and endeavors to cajole the ego into paths decreed by society's morals, customs, and laws. But this Freudian superego plays only a minor role, and the role of a meddler at that. Its function is defined mostly as interference with the desired direct expression of the libido. Such a negative interpretation of influence we must regard as inadequate. This is just the point where the deterministic theories of personality break down most obviously, for a denial of creative will and a consequent overemphasis on instinct make influence inexplicable.

10. The common practice of holding up Jesus as an ideal for youth is very much open to question. Serving Jesus and his cause is one thing; but trying to be another Jesus, or trying to assume his role in life as Savior, is a different thing and carries very dangerous and hypocritical implications. Religious educators who advise youth in the latter direction have missed, it is fair to say, the meaning of Jesus' teaching and Christianity. He is the Son of God, the Savior in a way qualitatively different from that open to other men, and his value to us is far greater than that of an ethical example. The more sound approach in our religious education is to explain the goals advocated by Christianity, such as unselfish service and brotherly living, and to hold these up before youth. To the extent that young people accept these goals for themselves, they will achieve empathy with the human element in Christ; and through this channel they will avail themselves of the influence which is desired. Jung puts the matter poignantly: "It is no easy matter to live a life that is modelled on Christ's, but it is unspeakably harder to live one's own life as truly as Christ lived his. . . . The modern man, moreover, is not eager to know in what way he can imitate Christ, but in what way he can live his own individual life, however meager and uninteresting it may be." (*Modern Man in Search of a Soul*, pp. 273, 274.)

11. "It is impossible," Adler points out, "to have a lasting influence upon an individual whom one is harming. One can influence another individual best when he is in the mood in which he feels his own rights guaranteed." (*Understanding Human Nature*, p. 63.)

12. *Modern Man in Search of a Soul*, p. 59.

CHAPTER V

1. Adler, *Understanding Human Nature*, p. 170.
2. I am using the term "character" to designate that external aspect of personality which is seen by the world.
3. Freud, *Psychopathology of Everyday Life*, p. 220.
4. Quoted by Adler, *Understanding Human Nature*, p. 252.
5. "We may deduce that all recollections have an unconscious purpose within themselves. They are not fortuitous phenomena, but speak clearly the language of encouragement or of warning. . . . We remember those events whose recollection is important for a specific

psychic tendency, because these recollections further an important underlying movement." (*Ibid*., pp. 48, 49.)

6. Adler's expression "style of life" means something very similar to our term "personality pattern," the chief difference being that "style of life" emphasizes the direction in which the individual is moving whereas "personality pattern" refers more to the adjustment of tensions within the individual which is the source of this movement.

7. Jones, an English psychoanalyst, says that the success of a psychotherapist can be judged by the number of personal belongings of his or her clients that accumulate in the therapist's office, as leaving something behind is an unconscious expression on the part of the patient of a desire to come back.

8. See Freud, *Psychopathology of Everyday Life*, and similar works by the other therapists.

9. See Chapter VIII in Adler's *Understanding Human Nature* for the best explanation of this subject.

CHAPTER VII

1. *General Introduction to Psychoanalysis*, p. 374.

   Adler likewise makes it clear that the decision must come from the patient: "The bringing about of a change in the nature of the patient can emanate from him alone. I always found it most profitable ostentatiously to sit with my hands in my lap, fully convinced the patient, no matter what I might be able to say on the point, as soon as he has recognized his life-line, can obtain nothing from me that he, as a sufferer, does not understand better." (*Practice and Theory of Individual Psychology*, p. 46.)

2. *Truth and Reality*, p. 41.

3. *Modern Man in Search of a Soul*, p. 260.

4. *Let's Be Normal*, p. 168.

5. Quoted by Elliott, *Solving Personal Problems*, p. 303.

CHAPTER VIII

1. *The Problem of Lay Analyses*, p. 11.

2. It goes without saying that this use of religion as a cloak for one's own ego striving is not the fault of the religion itself but rather of the neurotic tendencies of the individual who assumes the religion. A true understanding of religion would get over the neurosis, as we shall see in the final chapter.

3. In counseling with the type of person who endeavors to rule the specific sexual function out of his or her life, my question as to whether the counselee looks forward to marriage is often answered by, "Yes, I think it would be nice to have a home," or, "Yes, I want to have children." Both having a home and children are essential aspects of marriage, but either or both motives as the main foundation of marriage are dangerous. We normally expect love for a member of the opposite sex to be the central motive leading to marriage, and when this is absent we may expect that the sex problem has not been satisfactorily handled. This general attitude toward marriage may carry over into the plan of isolating sexual relations to the once or twice a year when the conception of children is desired. There is no question psychologically that this is a harmful and dangerous practice.
4. *Understanding Human Nature*, p. 264.
5. *Ibid.*, p. 157.
6. *Modern Man in Search of a Soul*, p. 270.

CHAPTER IX

1. *Understanding Human Nature*, p. 255.
2. Quoted from a letter of Rousseau by Hoffding, *Jean Jacques Rousseau and His Philosophy*, p. 76.
3. *Beyond Good and Evil*, p. 174.
4. Adler, *What Life Should Mean to You*, p. 262.

CHAPTER X

1. Freud, *The Future of an Illusion*, p. 52.
2. *Ibid.*, p. 76. Freud attacks religion unsparingly in this and others of his books. But this is Freud at his least astute, and his polemics do him no credit. His discussion of religion shows a misunderstanding of what religion is, and he falls into a morass of inconsistencies.
3. Freud emphasizes the neurotic aspects of philosophy and art as well as religion, whereas Rank calls them "the great spontaneous therapies of man." *Truth and Reality*, p. 88.
4. *Modern Man in Search of a Soul*, p. 264.
5. *Ibid.*, p. 261.
6. *Two Essays on Analytical Psychology*, p. 73.
7. *Modern Man in Search of a Soul*, p. 279.
8. *Psychology and Religion*, p. 99.

Jung explains how this primordial image of God springs up in modern persons by describing the case of one of his patients who experienced the recurrent fantasy of being held in the arms of a very large man, appearing to her like a father. This large man was standing in a field with the wind blowing about. In such a fantasy, Jung points out, we have the image of the father, the idea of support and protection, and the blowing of the wind, which symbolizes the "spirit" character of the fantasy. In other words, this is the image of God springing up in the patient's mind. "We are dealing with a genuine and really primitive divine-image, which grew in the unconscious of a modern mind and produced a living effect, an effect which both in respect to religion and psychology might cause one to reflect." (*Two Essays on Analytical Psychology*, p. 138.)

Jung also holds that creeds and dogma are expressions of archetypes, representing the classic formulations of fundamental and universal truths. "A creed is always the result and fruit of many minds and many centuries, purified from all oddities, shortcomings, and flaws of individual experience." (*Psychology and Religion*, p. 63.)

Religious experience does not need rational proof or substantiation, Jung holds. "Religious experience is absolute. It is indisputable. . . . No matter what the world thinks about religious experience, the one who has it possesses the great treasure of a thing that has provided him with a source of life, meaning, and beauty and that has given a new splendor to the world and to mankind." (*Ibid.*, p. 113.)

The healing of a neurosis is like a religious experience. "And if such experience helps to make your life healthier, more beautiful, more complete, and more satisfactory to yourself and to those you love, you may safely say: 'This was the grace of God.' " (*Ibid.*, p. 114.)

References

Adler, Alfred: *The Practice and Theory of Individual Psychology*. Translated by P. Radin. Harcourt, Brace and Co., New York, 1924.

———— *Understanding Human Nature*. Translated by Walter Beran Wolfe. Greenberg, New York, 1927.

———— *What Life Should Mean to You*. Edited by Alan Porter. Little, Brown and Co., Boston, 1931.

Elliott, H. S., and Elliott, G. L.: *Solving Personal Problems*. Henry Holt and Co., New York, 1937.

Freud, Sigmund: *The Future of an Illusion*. Translated by W. D. Robson-Scott. Horace Liveright, New York, 1928.

――― *A General Introduction to Psychoanalysis*. Authorized translation by G. Stanley Hall. Horace Liveright, New York, 1920.

――― *New Introductory Lectures on Psychoanalysis*. Translated by W. J. H. Sprott. W. W. Norton & Co., New York, 1933.

――― *The Problem of Lay-Analyses*. Translated by A. Paul Maerker-Brauden. Brentano's, New York, 1928.

――― *The Psychopathology of Everyday Life*. Authorized English edition, with introduction by A. A. Brill. Macmillan, New York, 1917.

Hoffding, H.: *Jean Jacques Rousseau and His Philosophy*. Translated by W. Richards and L. E. Saidla. Yale University Press, New Haven, 1930.

Jung, C. G.: *Modern Man in Search of a Soul*. Translated by W. S. Dell and C. F. Baynes. Harcourt, Brace and Co., New York, 1933.

――― *Psychology and Religion*. Yale University Press, New Haven, 1938.

――― *Psychological Types; or, The Psychology of Individuation*. Translated by H. Godwin Baynes. Harcourt, Brace and Co., New York, 1923.

――― *Two Essays in Analytical Psychology*. Translated by H. G. and C. F. Baynes. Dodd, Mead & Co., New York, 1928.

Levy-Bruhl, Lucien: *How Natives Think*. Authorized translation by Lilian A. Clare. George Allen & Unwin, London, 1926.

Mann, Thomas: *Freud, Goethe, Wagner*. Alfred A. Knopf, New York, 1937.

Nietzsche, Friedrich: *Beyond Good and Evil*. Translated by Helen Zimmern. London, 1909. The Modern Library, 1917.

Rank, Otto: *Truth and Reality*. Translated by Jessie Taft. Alfred A. Knopf, New York, 1936.

――― *Will Therapy*. Translated by Jessie Taft. Alfred A. Knopf, New York, 1936.

Rhine, J. B.: *New Frontiers of the Mind*. Farrar and Rinehart, New York, 1937.

Whitehead, A. N.: *The Function of Reason*. Princeton University Press, Princeton, 1929.

Index